THE JOY OF

SELF-CARE

250 DIY De-Stressors and Inspired Ideas Full of Comfort, Calm, and Relaxation

BECCA ANDERSON

CORAL GABLES

Copyright © 2022 by Becca Anderson.
Published by Mango Publishing, a division of Mango Publishing Group, Inc.

Cover Design & Art Direction: Morgane Leoni
Cover & Interior Illustrations: Ruslana/Adobe Stock
Layout & Design: Katia Mena

For permission requests, please contact the publisher at:
Mango Publishing Group
2850 S Douglas Road, 4th Floor
Coral Gables, FL 33134 USA
info@mango.bz

For special orders, quantity sales, course adoptions and corporate sales, please email the publisher at sales@mango.bz. For trade and wholesale sales, please contact Ingram Publisher Services at customer.service@ingramcontent.com or +1.800.509.4887.

The Joy of Self-Care: 250 DIY De-Stressors and Inspired Ideas Full of Comfort, Calm, and Relaxation

Library of Congress Cataloging-in-Publication number: Has been requested
ISBN: (print) 978-1-64250-924-3, (ebook) 978-1-64250-925-0
BISAC category code HEA055000, HEALTH & FITNESS / Mental Health

Printed in the United States of America

To those starting, growing, and evolving their
self-care journey.

❊ TABLE OF CONTENTS ❊

Introduction   8

CHAPTER ONE
Home Spa   13

CHAPTER TWO
Appreciate the Wonders of Nature   27

CHAPTER THREE
Time for DIY & Crafts   47

CHAPTER FOUR
Small, Personal Joys   67

CHAPTER FIVE
Spend Time with Loved Ones   83

CHAPTER SIX
Enhancing the Senses   99

CHAPTER SEVEN
Making Time for Rest   115

CHAPTER EIGHT
Reflecting on Life   **131**

CHAPTER NINE
Acts of Kindness   **147**

CHAPTER TEN
Essence of Self-Care   **163**

CHAPTER ELEVEN
Recipes to Savor   **185**

CHAPTER TWELVE
Seasonal Comforts   **211**

Self-Care Letter to Reader   230
About the Author   231

INTRODUCTION

Five years ago, I had a cold turned flu that left me
with a lingering cough, one that lasted for months. I
went to the doctor and faithfully took my prescribed
medications, but nothing got rid of my cough. Tired of
hearing myself hack, and with an aching, sore chest and
an inkling that I was irritating my coworkers with my
noise, I decided to take matters into my own hands.

I scanned a study on herbal teas and tonics sworn to
relieve bothersome coughs, and I embarked upon a
grand experiment of trying different pots of herbal
tea combinations every day to see which one would
do the trick and banish this oh so tiresome coughing
habit of mine.

After a few days, I found the golden elixir, whose
contents surprised me, being that they were apple,
chicory root, and chamomile. Only that combo seemed
to work its magic to soothe and calm the coughing.
After one week of drinking several pots of it a day, I was
cough-free.

Mind you, I am a diehard coffee lover, so shifting to
tea was a big deal for me, but I was grateful to have

made the switch when I started to notice other health benefits. On tea, I felt more hydrated, brighter in mood, and overall healthier.

I must confess I felt a bit of pride that I had been able to cure something doctors couldn't through a homely, kitchen cupboard approach to healing. This tiny self-care win encouraged me to pursue other aspects of healthy living. Rather than driving to the post office, I walked there to send my mail. Instead of getting in the car to get my beloved triple latte, I slipped on my sneakers to walk a mile or two for my coffee.

These small changes provided additional benefits such as a chance to increase my vitamin D intake, as well as more time to be calm and contemplative on my walks; and these centering walks helped me untangle little problems with work and gave me space to brainstorm writing projects while supporting an increase in my energy levels, allowing my brain to work better.

Just starting with those two simple self-care strategies has inspired me to take on a mindful approach to self-care and to make it a daily priority. I now ask myself, "How can I incorporate self-care into my workday?" and "How can I take better care of myself at every opportunity?"

This changed mindset led me to gather as many inspired ideas as possible to offer to you, dear reader.

We all have stressors in our lives, whether they stem from pressures caused by ongoing obligations or complications brought on by unexpected changes. We don't leap out of bed every morning into our stylish outfits fit for a pretty day; sometimes we might have the Monday morning blues, or maybe we feel strained or worn down just by thinking about our overstuffed to-do lists, which always seem to include more than we can tackle in one day.

When you feel this way, try the ideas in this book, which range from simple things to do in a moment to more thoughtful, easy DIY crafts and how-tos so you can live a more handmade life.

One of my fervent hopes for this book is that it will serve to connect you more to nature, whether it's planting oregano and basil for cooking, making lovely containers of succulents, growing herbs for tea, or

acquainting yourself with local trees or other treasures
of nature in your own backyard.

The purpose of the ideas here is to help you attain
a sense of serenity and calm contentment and
supplement your self-care routines, and by doing so,
boost your mood, immunity, and sense of self.

BECCA ANDERSON

CHAPTER ONE

—

HOME SPA

❋ HOMEMADE BUBBLE BATH ❋

Bubble bath is a great gift that even small kids can make. The trick here is twofold: Have a pretty container to put it in, and never divulge your ingredients.

- 2 CUPS IVORY (OR OTHER UNSCENTED) DISHWASHING LIQUID
- ⅛ OUNCE OF YOUR FAVORITE ESSENTIAL OIL (VANILLA IS MY FAVORITE)

Drop the oil into the dishwashing liquid and let sit covered for one week. Pour it into a beautiful bottle and add a ribbon, a gift tag, and instructions to use ¼ cup per bath. Makes enough for 8 baths.

❋ OATMEAL MASKS ❋

Masks are used to deep clean and condition the skin. They should be applied only after you have thoroughly washed your face, making sure to avoid your eyes as you apply the mask. After applying, lie down for fifteen minutes, covering your eyes with water moistened eye pads. The kind of mask you choose depends on your skin type. This one works for all types—and it's so easy to make.

- ½ CUP WATER
- ¼ CUP OATMEAL

Bring water to a boil, add oats, and cook over medium heat about 5 minutes, stirring occasionally. Allow to cool until warm but not hot. Apply to clean skin and leave on for 15 minutes. Rinse with warm water, then cool water, and pat dry.

❋ SKIN-SOOTHING BATH ❋

Here's a great bath recipe for the winter, when skin gets so dry.

- 1 CUP BUTTERMILK
- 3 TABLESPOONS EPSOM SALTS
- ½ TABLESPOON CANOLA OIL
- SOOTHING ESSENTIAL OIL OF YOUR CHOICE, SUCH AS LAVENDER OR CHAMOMILE

Combine ingredients and pour mixture into the stream of warm water as the tub is filling. Immerse yourself and relax for ten to fifteen minutes.

❋ SKIN SPRING CLEANING ❋

You can give your skin a great spring cleaning with all-natural products.

For oily skin: Combine 1 egg white with 1 tablespoon of oatmeal and mix well. Apply in a thin layer to face and neck and leave for 15 to 20 minutes. Egg white contains papain, a natural enzyme that eliminates subcutaneous dirt and oil; the oatmeal is rich in protein and potassium and will give your skin a vital mineral boost.

For dry skin: Spread a thin, even layer of honey on face and neck, taking care to avoid eyes. Honey is a natural humectant and traps moisture in the skin.

❊ HOMEMADE
ALPHA-HYDROXY MASK ❊

Cook half of a diced and peeled apple in ¼ cup of milk until soft and tender. Mash, then cool to room temperature; when cool, apply to skin. Thoroughly cleanse with warm water after 15 to 20 minutes.

❊ NATURAL HAIR CARE ❊

One simple, effective, old-fashioned hair rinse is good old vinegar, preferably cider vinegar. Mix 2 tablespoons in 2 cups of warm water. Work through hair after shampooing and rinsing, then rinse again with clear water. For light hair, use lemon juice instead of vinegar. This will help restore the natural acid balance of the scalp and get rid of all traces of soap and shampoo. For an all-purpose hair conditioner, combine ¾ cup olive oil, ½ cup honey, and the juice of 1 lemon. Rinse hair with water and towel dry. Work a small amount of conditioner into hair, comb through, and cover with a shower cap or plastic wrap for a half hour. Shampoo and rinse thoroughly. Store remaining conditioner in the refrigerator.

❋ MINIMALIST HOT TUB ❋

Hot tubs can be expensive and time-consuming. If you like the idea of bathing outside, consider buying an old-fashioned claw-foot tub (they cost about a thousand dollars and fit two people) for outside and run hot and cold water out to it from the house. Because you fill and drain the tub each time (letting water trickle into your garden afterwards rather than wasting it), you're spared the hassle and expense of chemicals.

❋ COOL AND SOOTHING ❋

When the weather is hot and sticky, refrigerate your facial toner, freshener, astringent, or aftershave. It will be as cool as the advertisements in the glossy magazines promise.

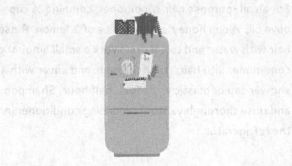

✳ RESTORATIVE BATH ✳

This bath a great pick-me-up.

- 1 COTTON BATH BAG OR PIECE
  OF CHEESECLOTH
- 2 TABLESPOONS GRATED FRESH GINGER
- 1 OUNCE FRESH ROSEMARY
- 20 DROPS ROSEMARY OIL
- 20 DROPS LAVENDER OIL
- 1 CUP ROSE WATER

Place the fresh ginger and rosemary in a cotton bath bag, or bundle in a one-foot-square piece of new cheesecloth, and tie it closed. Place the bag under the bathtub spigot and run hot water over it. Add oils and rose water to the bathtub, swirling with your hand to combine. The bath bag makes an excellent scrubber and exfoliator, and the ginger and rosemary will leave skin pleasantly tingling and feeling revived.

❄ EVERGREEN BATH SALTS ❄

Looking for an easy-to-make natural treat for a teacher or friend? Try these fabulous bath salts. They will be greatly appreciated.

- 2 CUPS KOSHER SALT
- 1 ATTRACTIVE GLASS JAR WITH TIGHT-FITTING LID
- 2 LARGE HANDFULS FRESH PINE NEEDLES (ONE OF THE LONGER VARIETIES)

Place 2 tablespoons salt evenly on the bottom of the jar. Lay 12 pine needles over the salt. Alternate salt and pine needles until the jar is full. Cover and place in a cool dark spot for four to six weeks. Add a pretty ribbon and gift tag. Makes 1 jar.

❄ PEACHES-AND-CREAM MOISTURIZER ❄

This lotion feels fabulous on the face. In a blender or a food processor, blend one peach and enough heavy cream to create a spreadable consistency. Massage onto your skin when needed. Refrigerate unused portion, and make sure to use it up within a day or so before it turns.

✻ SKIN-SOOTHER BATH ✻

This wonderful recipe will soothe any skin condition, from heat rash to chicken pox. It's wonderful for your skin and hair, so use it even when your skin feels fine!

- ½ CUP FINELY GROUND OATMEAL
- 1 CUP VIRGIN OLIVE OIL
- 2 CUPS ALOE VERA GEL
- 20 DROPS ROSEMARY OR LAVENDER OIL

Combine the ingredients in a large bowl; stir well. Add the mixture to a warm, running bath.

❋ BATH SALTS ❋

You can feel great by making bath salts for yourself or as gifts. Place 3 cups Epsom salts in a large bowl. In a measuring cup, combine 1 tablespoon glycerin, a few drops of food coloring, and a spray of your favorite perfume. Mix well and then slowly add the liquid mixture to the Epsom salts, stirring well. Pour into decorative glass jars and tie on a ribbon bow.

❋ WARM TOWELS ❋

Before getting into the shower, put a big, fluffy bath towel in the dryer. Let it get hot and then bring it into the bathroom with you when you take a shower. Better yet, get someone else to hand it to you directly from the dryer when you step out of the water.

❊ PINE POTPOURRI ❊

This spicy concoction evokes the smell of the deep woods.

- 1 QUART DRIED PINE NEEDLES
- 1½ TEASPOONS OF AN ESSENTIAL OIL SUCH AS PINE OR FIR
- 1 CUP CHOPPED PATCHOULI LEAVES (OR SUBSTITUTE CEDARWOOD CHIPS OR SHAVINGS)
- ½ CUP CINNAMON STICKS, BROKEN IN HALVES
- 1 TABLESPOON EACH WHOLE ALLSPICE, CINNAMON, CLOVES, AND MACE
- HANDFUL OF DRIED CRANBERRIES
- OPTIONAL: 1 TABLESPOON DRIED ORRIS ROOT, IN SMALL CHUNKS

Combine the pine needles and oil in a large bowl, then add rest of ingredients. Place in potpourri jars or a glass bowl.

❋ SLEEPY-TIME POTPOURRI ❋

For help with sleeping, try this potpourri in your
bedroom. The lavender is said to dispel melancholy,
the rosemary alleviates nightmares, and the chamomile
and marjoram act as soporifics, relaxing you in
body and mind.

- 2 CUPS LAVENDER FLOWERS
- 2 CUPS ROSEMARY (FLOWERS AND LEAVES)
- 1 CUP CHAMOMILE FLOWERS
- 2 TABLESPOONS MARJORAM
- 2 TEASPOONS ANISEED
- 5 DROPS BERGAMOT OIL
- OPTIONAL: 2 TEASPOONS ORRIS ROOT CHIPS

Mix all ingredients together and place in a favorite bowl;
you can also fill small sachet bags to hang near you.

❃ COZY UP ❃

No hot water bottle or heating pad handy? Try
moistening a thick hand towel or a modest-sized bath
towel, folding it, then heating it in a microwave oven for
about 1 minute and 30 seconds, looking in on it every
30 seconds. Check to make sure it's not too hot, then
press this "moist heat" pad on aching muscles. When
it cools down, reheat for about 30 seconds. Use a face
towel for smaller aches.

Here's a dry version. Take a clean, heavyweight sock
such as a cotton tube sock. Fill halfway with 4 to 5 cups
of raw rice. Tie a knot in the top of the sock or wrap
string around it and tie firmly. Warm in the microwave
for 30 seconds at a time until it's the right temperature.
This heating pad will reshape itself to fit against
sore muscles, especially sore necks. Take care not to
get it wet.

CHAPTER TWO

-

APPRECIATE
THE WONDERS
OF NATURE

❋ CACTUS GARDEN ❋

This makes a perfect gift for those who want plants but tend to kill them by not watering them. Find a low ceramic pot or bowl and plant a few different varieties of cactus in it. You might want to add a pretty rock or some dried flowers for color (red celosia is a wonderful choice). Handling a cactus doesn't have to be painful if you wrap a towel around it several times and use the towel like a hoist to gently lift it out of the old pot and into the new. Rather than using your fingers, use a spoon to pack dirt around roots.

❋ INDOOR GARDENS ❋

In the winter when my garden is dry and bare, nothing gives me more pleasure than a visit to the local garden shop, where it always feels like sweet, balmy summer. I wander through the rows of brightly colored flowers and gleaming, richly hued leaves, and the aroma of blossoms and sweet rich earth make me forget the outdoor gloom and blustery weather for a time. The plants and flowers are completely oblivious to the weather outside, and their verdant outbursts of energy restore mine. I take an inordinate amount of time picking out some ridiculously expensive and riotously colored plant that just screams warm weather, which I then take home and place on my windowsill or bedside table in a beautiful basket or brightly colored cachepot. I kind of have a "brown thumb," so my plants never last long; but I almost prefer that, as it gives me a chance to go to the garden shop again that much sooner!

❊ ROSEMARY WREATH ❊

Rosemary grows in abundance in many parts of the country. I love to use it fresh, so I've learned to make this simple rosemary heart to hang in my kitchen. I just tear off sprigs as I need them. If I don't use it fast enough, no problem—it's just as tasty dried.

To make your own rosemary wreath, you will need:

- 3 FEET GARDEN WIRE
- FLORAL WIRE (THE GREEN–FLOCKED KIND LOOKS BEST)
- 12 LONG STEMS ROSEMARY

Make a hook at the end of the wire, then bend the wire into a heart shape and hook the ends together. Starting at the top, attach a stem of rosemary to the wire with floral wire so that its leafy top points into the middle. Repeat on the other side. Then wire stems down both sides and join them at the bottom. Makes 1 wreath.

✿ FLOWER FRAMES ✿

You can beautify family photos by matting them with mat boards in attractive colors and then gluing on dried flowers. A great gift! You will need:

- MAT BOARDS
- SPANISH MOSS
- DRIED FLOWERS
- GLUE GUN

Find mat boards that fit the photos you want to frame; you can have them cut to size at many art supply stores. Arrange the moss and flowers in an attractive pattern on the mat board, and then hot glue in place.

❊ MAD FOR MUSHROOMS ❊

Gardeners who need a farming fix during the cold winter months should consider a mushroom kit. These kits come in a number of varieties, including shiitake and button mushrooms. The kits contain a sterilized, enriched growing medium that is preinoculated with mushroom spores that can easily be grown indoors in a cool, dark place year-round.

❊ COAXING SPRING ❊

When you've got the winter blahs, one of the easiest cures is to anticipate spring and bring a bit of color indoors by forcing branches to blossom early. Any of a wide variety of bushes, shrubs, and trees will do, including forsythia, crab apple, pussy willows, quince, cherry, plum, pear, dogwood, privet, red maple, gooseberry, weeping willow, and witch hazel. Simply cut the ends of the branches on a slant with sharp scissors and immediately plunge the ends into a vase of warm water. (The water should not be too warm for you to touch.) As the days pass, make sure to keep the vases filled with plenty of clean, tepid water, and the warmth of the house will do the rest of the work. Voilà—instant spring!

❋ INDOOR GREENERY ❋

When it's gray and dreary outside, I like to plant an indoor kitchen garden in a sunny window. One of my favorites is a lemon herb garden, because it lends such a tart, fresh fragrance to the room. You can either put plants in one long container or use a variety of small pots. Choose from lemon basil, lemon verbena, lemon thyme, lemon balm, lemon geranium, and lemongrass to fill the air with the delicious, tangy scent of citrus. Treat these plants to plenty of sun and well-drained soil. Be sure to pick the blooms from lemon verbena and lemon basil when they flower. The more you pick and use these herbs, the more prolific the plants will be. Consider mixing in a yellow flowering plant to visually highlight the lemon fragrance. What to do with all this lemon flavor? Try making lemon honey: Coarsely chop ½ cup lemon balm or lemon verbena and place in a saucepan with 1 cup honey. Over low heat, simmer on low heat for 20 minutes, then strain out herbs and store honey in a container with a tight lid. Or you may also want to make lemon butter: Soften ½ cup butter, then combine in a small bowl with 2 tablespoons of finely chopped lemon basil or lemon thyme. This savory lemon herb butter is great for seafood and pasta.

❊ EASY HERBAL BOUQUET ❊

When purchasing fresh herbs, cut off the bottoms and place them in a nice vase on the kitchen sill. This not only brightens up the kitchen, it also adds fragrance, keeps the herbs fresher longer, and it has the added benefit of visually reminding you to use them in a variety of dishes.

❋ ONION AND
GARLIC BRAIDS ❋

I love to grow onions and garlic just so that I can braid them into garlands and give them as presents. All you have to do in preparation is to leave on the long tops when you harvest your crop. Making these garlands is just like braiding hair. Cut a piece of twine as long as you want your braid to be and lay it on a table. Line up the onions or garlic in a row on the twine with all of the green tops toward you, with each onion or garlic bulb slightly overlapping the one before. Starting with the one at the top of the line, separate the leaves into three sections, incorporating the twine into one of the sections, and braid the three sections together. When you are about halfway down the length of the first bulb's leaves, begin to incorporate the second bulb's leaves so that the bulb sits on top of the previous braid. Continue until you reach the end of the bulbs. Dry in the sun for 3 to 5 days, and then they are ready for hanging as decorations—and to use. Simply snip off the last one on the braid as needed.

✳ GIVING BIRDS A HOME ✳

Birds really do like birdhouses, as long as you
make them hospitable. Make a birdhouse fit into its
surroundings both in color and texture as much as
possible (twigs, bark, and unpainted materials are best;
birds don't want to feel as if they are on display). Place
any house at least six feet off the ground and away
from foot and cat traffic. Face it away from the sun,
preferably in trees or shrubs. Don't despair if birds
don't move in till the second year the house is there;
they need time to get used to it. One easy bird-friendly
option is to buy a standard birdhouse at a store and
hot glue straw or dried grasses to the roof, creating a
natural thatched effect.

✳ HAND-PICKED
LETTUCE MIXES ✳

Are you a fan of those expensive mixed salad greens?
You can easily make your own mix by buying lettuce
seeds such as oak leaf, black seeded simpson, and red
salad bowl, as well as arugula, mizuna, watercress,
and chicory. In many parts of the country, it is too hot

to grow lettuce during the summer. But you can still successfully keep them going even during the summer if you plant new seedlings every few weeks and provide a "roof" made of shade cloth you can buy at any garden supply store. The trick is to harvest when the leaves are very young and tender, otherwise they may become too bitter. When the plants are a few inches high, sheer off the tops with scissors; they will grow back quickly, and you'll have salads for weeks.

❋ WILDFLOWER MEADOW ❋

I don't know about you, but I believe lawns are vastly overrated. They require a tremendous amount of water and too much labor, and they cause vast quantities of chemicals to be dumped into our water supply. So I decided to dig mine up and plant a wildflower meadow instead. It took some work to get it going, but within four weeks, I had my first bloom. It was a glorious sight for six months, and unlike a lawn, virtually maintenance free. Plus, I had an almost endless supply of cut flowers from late spring to late fall. The tricks are to till the soil in the spring, select a pure wildflower mix of seeds (with no grass or vermiculite filler) appropriate to your area, and blend the seed with four times its volume of fine sand so it will disperse evenly. After you've spread it over the dirt, lay down a layer of loose hay to keep the seeds from blowing away. Usually, wildflower seed mixes are a combination of annuals, biannuals, and perennials. To keep the annuals going every year, rough up parts of the soil and just reseed those flowers.

❉ SPROUTS IN A JAR ❉

Raw sprouts are a wonderful source of vitamins. Any beans—soy, fava, lima, pinto, garbanzo, lentils, peas, and more—can be sprouted, as can alfalfa, sunflower, buckwheat, and many other seeds. Just be sure never to try potatoes or tomatoes—the sprouts are poisonous. And don't sprout seeds that have been sold for garden planting; they've probably been treated with a fungicide. Untreated seeds for sprouting are available at health food stores.

- 2 TABLESPOONS ALFALFA SEEDS
- 1 WIDE-MOUTH ONE-QUART JAR
- WATER
- CHEESECLOTH
- RUBBER BAND

Place the seeds in the bottom of the jar and fill the jar with water. Put cheesecloth over the top and secure with a rubber band. Store in a warm, dark place such as a kitchen cupboard. Two or three times a day take the jar out, empty the water, and add new water. The sprouts will be ready in 4 to 5 days and will keep up to a week in the refrigerator. Makes 1 quart.

❋ TIME FOR THYME ❋

Grow a yard of woolly thyme instead of grass. Not only is it easier to care for and (virtually) never in need of watering, it will hold the heat of the day's sun and fill your yard with a singularly pleasing smell. At the very least, try it between the stones or bricks of your front walk or garden path. Every time you walk across it, the smell will waft up. (And you can use it in any recipe that calls for thyme.)

❋ FLOWER TIEBACKS ❋

I love the romantic look of lace curtains in my bedroom. Recently I came across wonderful rose tiebacks that are quite easy to make and look great against the lacy fabric. They're delicate, so once they are on the curtains, try to avoid taking them off and putting them back on all the time.

- HALF-INCH-THICK SATIN RIBBON
- MOSS
- SMALL DRIED ROSES

Tie a length of ribbon around the curtain you want to tie back and cut to correct length, leaving some extra for the tying process. Mark the area that covers the front with two straight pins, one on either end, then take each ribbon off the curtain to add decoration to it. Glue small pieces of moss to the area between the two pins. Glue roses attractively into the moss. With scissors, trim away any unsightly moss. Tie onto curtain; trim the ends of the ribbon afterward if they end up too long. Repeat to make as many tiebacks as needed.

❋ DAISY CHAINS ❋

I grew up next to a field where all sorts of wildflowers bloomed—daisies and black-eyed Susans, buttercups and Queen Anne's lace. One of my favorite things to do on lazy summer afternoons was to collect daisies and make a chain. Sometimes I would wear the chain in my hair, and at other times, I might festoon the headboard in my bedroom with it, or I might offer it as a present to my mother. I still remember how to make one. The trick is to cut the daisies with long stems (one foot). You start with three blooms on a flat surface—the ground is just fine—staggered at various heights. Braid these together. Then add a fourth daisy to the center of the three and braid it into the chain. Continue as long as you have daisies, time, and patience. Tie off the end with a knot.

❋ PRODUCE FOR APARTMENT DWELLERS ❋

If you have no space or time for a garden (or are plagued by critters eating your goodies before you get to harvest them), try creating hanging vegetable baskets. According to experts, almost anything can be grown in a basket, but be sure to get compact growing varieties of the vegetables you want. Buy fourteen-inch diameter wire baskets (sixteen-inch for zucchini or mini watermelons). It's best to grow one type of vegetable per basket, although a variety of lettuces or herbs will work well together. Line basket with sphagnum moss and fill with potting soil. Plant seedlings rather than seeds, and hang the baskets outdoors from patios or rafters, locating them where they will get at least four hours of afternoon sun. Avoid overwatering seedlings, but once they become established, you do need to feed and water frequently; on the hottest days, they may even need to be watered twice daily. Once seedlings are three weeks old, fertilize every three weeks with an all-purpose soluble fertilizer, but never feed unless the soil is damp.

❋ COLORFUL DRIED HERBS ❋

When you dry your own herbs, they don't have to turn black or brown. Try this simple trick: Put freshly cut herbs that have been washed and well dried into a paper lunch bag, close the bag with a clothespin, and punch holes in four different places in the bag with a fork. Put the bag in the refrigerator. Each morning when you first open the fridge, give the bag a shake and turn it over. When the herbs are completely dry, store in a container until ready to use. Your parsley, chives, and so on will be bright green all year long!

❃ PRESSED FLOWERS ❃

Making pressed flowers is incredibly easy. It requires no special equipment and costs absolutely nothing. All you need is a heavy book. Find a meadow and collect small bouquets of wildflowers. Lay them flat in different parts of the book; if you are concerned about discoloration of the book's pages, place pieces of plain paper covering the pages and lay the flowers in the book between the pieces of paper. Place a small boulder (or anything else that's heavy and not likely to fall) on top of the book. Let sit for a few months.

❀ PRESSED-FLOWER
PAPERWEIGHTS ❀

These paperweights are truly a simple pleasure. Make
some pressed flowers and buy a hollow glass mold
at a craft store. Trace the bottom of the mold onto a
piece of mat board. Cut out the mat, then arrange the
pressed flowers on it and glue them in place. Hot glue
the glass mold to the mat; when dry, glue a circle of felt
to the bottom.

❀ WEED ARRANGING ❀

You don't need a flower garden to create beautiful
arrangements. All you need is access to a field and a bit
of imagination. Wild Queen Anne's lace, bittersweet,
winter cress, sea grape leaves, chive flowers, wild
mustard, thistles, horsetails, and goldenrod all look
wonderful in a simple vase; your arrangement can
either be all of one variety or a combination. Even the
simplicity of dried grasses or bare willow branches
can be beautiful, while various seed pods can make
extraordinary decorations when dried.

❋ HANDY GARDEN HINTS ❋

During growing season, many plants need to be staked—tomatoes, hollyhocks, and so on. Try tying them up with old pantyhose, which are soft enough not to cut into the stems of the plants.

If you want to capture seeds from this year's plants, zip small resealable plastic bags with tiny holes in them over the stems as the pods begin to form. (The holes will allow seeds to dry.) Remove when seeds are completely dry.

To remove the kernels on ears of corn for canning, drying, or just eating without cutting yourself, take a four-inch piece of wood, drive a long nail through the board, and spear the ear upright on the nail. It will be easy to cut in this position.

CHAPTER THREE

TIME FOR DIY & CRAFTS

❊ PAINT WITH PASSION ❊

Are you looking for an inexpensive way to jazz up your house? Add character to a room by painting the trim an unconventional color. If you are so inspired, consider the following:

1. STAY AWAY FROM TRENDY COLORS. YOU'RE PROBABLY GOING TO BE LIVING WITH THEM FOR A LONG TIME, AND YOU MIGHT JUST WANT SOMETHING DIFFERENT FROM WHAT EVERYONE ELSE HAS.
2. DON'T BE AFRAID TO MESS UP. YOU CAN ALWAYS PAINT OVER IT.
3. THINK ABOUT THE SURROUNDING ACCENT COLORS. WILL THEY MESH WITH THE NEW COLOR YOU'VE CHOSEN?

❋ CANDLE COLLARS ❋

A wonderful way to dress up pillar candles is to make
a candle collar. The candle must be fat enough to be
safe from toppling over, and you should never leave it
unattended. Make sure you place the candle on a dish
so that the hot wax won't spread all over and snuff out
the candle, with an inch of uncovered candle left at the
bottom of the collar to avoid accidents.

- BAY LEAVES, MAGNOLIA LEAVES, OR OTHER
  ATTRACTIVE OVAL–SHAPED LEAVES
- GLUE GUN
- PILLAR CANDLE
- RAFFIA

Put a little glue on the back of each leaf near the base
and press firmly to the candle. Trim the bottom of
the leaves so that the candle stands evenly. Tie raffia
around in a bow. Makes 1 candle.

❋ HOMEMADE FIRE STARTERS ❋

Here's a great gift for anyone with a fireplace
or woodstove.

- 1 BLOCK PARAFFIN
- FOOD DYE
- PINE OR CEDAR ESSENTIAL OIL
- SEVERAL MEDIUM OR LARGE PINECONES
- OLD TONGS
- WAXED PAPER

Melt the paraffin in the top of a double boiler. Add dye
of your choice to color the wax and a few drops of pine
or cedar essential oil to scent it. Stir with an old wooden
spoon. Using tongs, dip pinecones in wax to cover, and
then set on waxed paper to cool and harden.

❋ HOMEMADE STICKERS ❋

If you have kids under the age of twelve, chances are
they love stickers (which can be mighty expensive).
But you can make your own by turning any picture you
want into a sticker. First, collect appropriate images—

magazines headed for the recycling are one excellent source. Then, in a small cup, mix 2 parts white glue and 1 part vinegar. Use a small paintbrush to brush the mixture on the back of the picture. Let dry 1 hour, then cut, lick, and stick anytime you want to place them. The advantage to homemade stickers is that the kids will have a ball making them!

❋ FLOWER BARRETTES ❋

These are wonderful for people of all ages. You will need:

- PLAIN PLASTIC OR FLAT METAL HAIR BARRETTES
- SMALL DRIED FLOWERS (SMALL ROSE BUDS AND BABY'S BREATH ARE NICE)
- GLUE GUN

Decide on a pleasing arrangement, and hot glue the flowers onto the barrettes.

❋ ART PILLOW ❋

You can't needlepoint, quilt, sew, or crochet? Don't worry: making a one-of-a-kind pillow for your living room is as easy as pie—all you need is a drawing that you or your child has done and a few items from a fabric store.

- 1 DRAWING
- 1 PILLOW-SIZED PIECE OF FOAM (CHOOSE THE SIZE YOU'D LIKE THE PILLOW TO BE)
- 2 PIECES OF PLAIN FABRIC, EACH AN INCH LARGER AROUND THAN THE FOAM
- TRACING PAPER
- LIQUID EMBROIDERY (AVAILABLE AT CRAFT STORES)
- NEEDLE AND THREAD

Trace the drawing onto one of the pieces of fabric. Using the liquid embroidery, embroider the lines of the drawing onto the fabric. Place the two pieces of fabric together inside out and sew on three sides. Turn the pillow cover right side out, insert the foam, and then stitch the fourth side.

✿ DECORATIVE CHOKER ✿

Dressing up in all your finery is fun, especially when the weather turns warm. This easy-to-make necklace is perfect for everyone of all ages.

- VELVET RIBBON
- ONE INCH OF SELF-STICK VELCRO (SHOULD BE THE SAME COLOR AS THE RIBBON)
- SCISSORS
- DRIED FLOWER
- SPRAY CRAFT GLAZE
- HOT GLUE

Measure the neck size of the wearer. Add one inch to the neck size and cut the ribbon to this length. Take the fuzzy cloth side of the Velcro and attach it to one end of the ribbon (if the backing is not strong enough to stick to the ribbon, use a drop of hot glue, or alternatively, stitch it onto the ribbon). Take the plastic side of the Velcro and cut it in half. Attach this to the backside of the other end of the ribbon. Make sure that when you wrap the ribbon around the person's neck the Velcro catches. Take the dried flower and spray the head with the glaze to protect it. After it has dried, cut off the stem. Hot glue the flower to the center of the ribbon.

❋ RESTORE A PIECE
OF FURNITURE ❋

Because so many of us work primarily with our heads,
doing something with our hands can be tremendously
satisfying. I have an old pine blanket chest that I bought
about twenty years ago. Over the years, it has endured
dog scratches, children's scribbles, and scrapes from
candleholders. One day, I decided it needed some
help. So I sanded it down a bit and applied coat after
coat of Briwax and then cream furniture polish. Now
it glows again, and I smile every time I walk into the
room. Find something with intrinsic quality and value.
If someone once cared about the piece, no matter
how many layers of disguising paint and neglect it has
endured, you can restore it. Enjoy your creativity and a
sense of preserving the past, or do what my coworker
Brenda does: find a junky wooden or metal chair that
is being thrown away and save it from the landfill. Use
your imagination and paint it to create a one-of-a-kind
utilitarian artwork. Each leg a different color? The sky
on the seat? Let your imagination soar.

❋ FLOATING CANDLES ❋

Candles add a magical element to any room. I especially love using the floating ones as a centerpiece for the dining room table, solving the problem of having an overlarge arrangement that interferes with conversation. Simple float a few candles and some flowers in a bowl, and you have an elegant focal point. Fortunately, small floating candles are not difficult to make, and this way, you can decide exactly what aroma you'd like them to send forth.

- 12 OUNCES PARAFFIN
- 60 DROPS OF YOUR FAVORITE ESSENTIAL OIL
- 12 ONE-INCH FLOATING CANDLEWICKS (AVAILABLE AT CRAFT STORES)
- 12 SMALL METAL PASTRY TINS OR CANDLE MOLDS

In a double boiler, melt the paraffin, then add the essential oil with a wooden spoon. Pour wax into molds slowly to avoid air bubbles. Let half set, and then insert wicks in the center of each. Let candles set fully before unmolding. Makes 1 dozen.

❋ LACY BEAUTY ❋

Make lace napkin rings for your cloth napkins; you will
need perhaps a yard of one-inch-wide lace in a shade
that you like. Simply roll the napkins and tie each with
six inches or so of lace. Trim the edges of the lace for a
finished look.

❋ CANDLE POTS ❋

One of the easiest and most attractive arrangements
you can make for a table or sideboard is a series of
cream or white pillar candles in terra-cotta pots.
Just group them attractively, and you have a simple
yet sophisticated feeling. Make sure you never leave
candles unattended; the moss can catch on fire if the
candle burns too far down.

- DRY FLORAL FOAM
- 1 TERRA-COTTA POT
- 1 PILLAR CANDLE
- GLUE GUN
- GREEN, SPHAGNUM, OR REINDEER MOSS
- FLORAL OR STRAIGHT PINS

Trim the foam to approximately the same shape as the pot, making sure it is a little larger than the pot's diameter. Push the foam firmly into the pot until it touches the bottom. Trim if needed to get a good fit. Pack the spaces between the edge of the foam and the inside of the pot with moss. Trim the top of the foam so it is level with the top of the pot, then glue the candle to the foam. Surround base of candle with moss, fixing it in place with pins. Makes 1.

❋ EGGSHELL PLANTERS ❋

Ordinary eggshells make beautiful planters for small herbs or grasses. Break raw eggs, leaving shell at least half intact. Empty the contents into a separate bowl, then rinse the shell thoroughly. Place already sprouting plants in the shells, anchored with a bit of topsoil; mint, lavender, chives, or sage work well, as do wheat grass, alfalfa, or very small ferns. Cushion an assortment of shells and plants in moss and place in a beribboned basket or pot. Experiment with using dyed or decorated eggshells.

❋ THE ART ROOM ❋

Our family room is a bit different from most people's. It's a corner of a big closed-in porch that we have turned into an art corner. It has a large old table and chairs and a cabinet full of art supplies—paints, glue, paper of all sorts, glitter, Popsicle sticks, pipe cleaners, and dried flowers. Sometimes individually and sometimes together, the three of us—mother, father, and daughter—go in there to create something. We make cards, pictures to hang on the walls, and presents for one another and for other relatives. It's a place where each of us can express our creativity. I love to go in there with my three-year-old and fingerpaint, letting the goopy paint squish through my fingers and seeing what color combinations I can create from the three primary colors. Such a simple pleasure!

❋ PERSONALIZED NAPKIN RINGS ❋

At the craft store, buy a set of clear Lucite napkin rings (the kind with an opening that allows you to put a piece of paper inside). Cut paper to fit inside the rings. Glue pressed flowers onto the paper in any pleasing arrangement, then cover the paper with clear, heavy tape such as packing tape. Insert the paper into the rings. If you can't find Lucite napkin rings, you can glue pressed flowers directly onto wooden rings, then give them several coats of shellac.

❋ HOMEMADE PLAY-DOUGH ❋

This preschool staple is easy to make in batches at home. It's worth keeping an assortment of bottled food coloring for projects like these, even if you don't use them often for cooking.

- 1 CUP SALT
- 1¼ CUPS WATER
- 2 TEASPOONS VEGETABLE OIL
- 3 CUPS ALL-PURPOSE FLOUR (NOT SELF-RISING)
- 2 TABLESPOONS CORNSTARCH
- FOOD COLORING

In a large bowl, mix salt, water, and vegetable oil. Continue mixing while adding flour and cornstarch. Knead until smooth. If dough seems too sticky, add a little flour; if too dry, add a little water. Divide the dough into several lumps. Add a few drops of food coloring to each lump and knead to mix the color into the dough. Store in airtight containers; the dough will dry out if exposed to air.

❈ GARDENING SOAP ❈

Ever wonder what to do with all those slivers of soap?
I slip them into the leg of an old pair of pantyhose, clip
the leg off, and tie it to my spigot outside. Now I have a
convenient place to wash my hands after gardening.

❈ HANDMADE TRIVETS ❈

This is a great craft idea that is simplicity itself. Buy a
plain white or terra-cotta tile from a craft store. Draw a
design on it with a china-graph pencil (available at craft
stores)—little kids can do handprints, which are always
relished by doting parents. Then paint in your design
using model paints. When completely dry, coat it with
plain ceramic varnish.

❋ NATURAL PLACEMATS ❋

For your next party, use fall leaves as place cards and mats. First dip them in warm soapy water, rinse, and allow to air dry. Then press them between the leaves of a heavy book, allowing at least a week drying time. Make sure you end up with at least one dry leaf for each guest's place cards, plus several more for each placemat. When you remove the leaves, handle them carefully because they can easily tear. Using a gold marker, carefully write the name of each person on a leaf and place on table. Create a bed of leaves at each place for a placemat.

❋ HANDMADE BOOKMARKS ❋

For an elegant gift, try making bookmarks out of
ribbons and beads. Choose a pretty ribbon that's at
least an inch wide; velvet, brocade, and tapestry styles
are nice. Trim the top with pinking shears to keep it
from unraveling. Fold up the end of the ribbon to make
a point. Tack the ends together with a couple of secure
stitches in a matching thread. Sew a bead or charm onto
the end of the point to weight the bookmark and add a
pretty accent.

❋ NATURAL NUANCES ❋

The next time you host a party, lend a special touch
to your table with uniquely decorated and easy place
cards. For inspiration, look to the great outdoors!
Collect small pinecones, berry clusters, crab apples,
pretty leaves, or other natural ornaments. Create a card
for each guest, and use a pretty ribbon or piece of raffia
to attach the cards to your natural treasures. Place one
at each setting.

❋ PINECONE BIRD FEEDER ❋

This makes a great gift to the birds.

- 2 LARGE PINECONES
- TWINE OR RED RIBBON
- HOT GLUE GUN
- ½ CUP PEANUT BUTTER
- 1 FIFTEEN–OUNCE PACKAGE OF BIRD SEED
- 2 BOWLS, ONE MEDIUM, ONE LARGE
- 2 MIXING SPOONS
- OPTIONAL: SMALL SCREW HOOKS

Hot glue the twine or ribbon directly to the stems of the pinecones; if the stems are long enough, the cord or ribbon can also be tied to attach it to each pinecone even more securely. Put the peanut butter into the medium bowl and the bird seed into the large bowl. Place a cone into the peanut butter and roll it around, pushing the peanut butter onto the cone with a mixing spoon. When the pinecone is well covered, dip it into the bird seed. Roll it around, pressing the seed onto the cone with the second spoon until well covered. Hang from a tree limb. Makes 2.

❋ GREEN CHEER ❋

A green plant is a wonderful happiness booster. One
of the hardiest and easiest-to-grow plants is a sweet
potato. Even if you think you have a black thumb, try
it— sweet potatoes grow fast and are almost impossible
to kill. (OK, you *do* have to keep the glass full of
water, but that's it.) Get an old glass jar (a cleaned-out
spaghetti sauce jar is just right) and fill it with water.
Buy a sweet potato at the grocery store, and with the
ends of the sweet potato pointing up and down, poke
four toothpicks in the center as if you were marking
the four directions (north, south, east, and west); then
place the bottom half of the sweet potato in the water.
(The toothpicks will keep the whole potato from being
submerged.) Place in a sunny window and wait, adding
water if necessary. Soon you'll have lovely vines and big
curving leaves gracing your sill.

CHAPTER FOUR

-

SMALL,
PERSONAL JOYS

❋ CREATE A SIMPLE PLEASURES LIST ❋

What little things bring you joy? They're different for each of us. Here is my friend Pat's list:

1. WHEN I REALLY FEEL LISTENED TO
2. HAVING I THE BED ALL TO MYSELF
3. TAKING A HOT BUBBLE BATH
4. WHEN MY SON GIVES ME A BIG HUG AND HOLDS ON TIGHT

Make your own list—and then be sure to indulge regularly.

❋ CLEAN UP ❋

In talking with my friends and family, I always ask what they actually enjoy cleaning—what gives them energy and excitement to polish up. People mentioned straightening the tools in the garage, cleaning their desks before starting a new project, organizing the sock drawer once a year and throwing out all the single socks, and tackling the kitchen utensil drawer. What do you love to tidy or straighten up in your life? Give yourself a clean-up lift today.

❋ THE LANGUAGE OF LOVE ❋

Words do make the mood. We all know the usual terms of endearment: honey, dear, sweetie, and angel, to name but a few. But to fan the flames of ardor and romance, why not try some less tired language, like sweeting, sweetling, or sweetkin (terms in vogue in the sixteenth and seventeenth centuries)? Or how about dearling (the original form of darling)? Your partner could become your paramour (literally "through love" in French). Instead of attractive or cute, you could try toothsome or cuddlesome. Rather than just missing your beloved, try yearning, pining, longing, or hungering, and watch the passion build.

✳ I COULD HAVE DANCED
ALL NIGHT ✳

This is something I do only when I'm alone. I put old
Bob Marley tapes on my stereo and dance by myself in
the living room. Sometimes I watch myself in the mirror.
But mostly I dance with my eyes closed, just feeling
the music as it moves through my body. Of course,
you need to pick the music and the circumstances
that are just right for you. Give it a try and see how it
makes you feel.

✳ GO WILD–AT LEAST
A LITTLE ✳

Sometimes we just need to shake up our routines. What
little outrageous thing can you do today? Dye your hair?
Paint your toenails green? Play hooky from work? For

years, I lived near a street that must have had six or seven Chinese restaurants, and over time, I've probably eaten at them all. One day, I commented to my husband that each seemed to do a particular dish well and that putting them all together would make a great meal. So one night when we were feeling the need to be a bit outrageous, we did just that. We had potstickers from one place, then moved onto the next for hot and sour soup, a third for the Szechwan beef, and a fourth for the garlic eggplant. If anyone thought we were weird only ordering one item per restaurant, no one said anything. We had a ball—not to mention a great dinner.

❋ CARPE DIEM ❋

My father was an old-fashioned country doctor who made house calls and visited his patients in the county hospital every day except Sunday. On Saturdays, he would get up early, and on the way to the hospital, he'd stop for breakfast at what my mother always referred to as "the dirty diner." It was a greasy spoon in an old railroad car with split black leather booths whose chief appeal to my dad was the break in his routine of coffee and the newspaper before rushing off to work. I too

have learned the pleasure of having a special breakfast.
It's a chance to slow down and observe the start of the
day through new eyes. Also, eating a good breakfast is
good for you both mentally and physically. So perhaps
eat your breakfast in a different and special spot. You
can still read the newspaper, but remember to listen
to new sounds and really tune into the day, all while
enjoying the smells only breakfast provides.

❋ EAT WHAT YOU WANT ❋

I have a confession: I love Coca-Cola, as in six-cans-
a-day-if-I-didn't-control-myself. For many years
after my college Coke bingeing, I resisted altogether.
Then I married someone with the same secret passion,
and it crept back into the house. I wavered, worried,
and finally decided that I could enjoy one Coke a day
at most, no more. And I've kept to my commitment for
years. Many days I have none, but when I do choose
to have one, I really enjoy it. I drink it consciously,
noticing the bubbles as it goes down my throat and
the cold sweetness on my tongue. I savor my Coke,
wringing every drop of pleasure out of it. Just for today,
indulge your innocent craving (this is not permission for

alcoholics to drink, food addicts to eat, or ex-potheads to smoke; I'm talking harmless nonaddictive pleasures): the Chunky Monkey ice cream; the chocolate cake with mocha frosting; the bananas with peanut butter. Whatever it is that you love to eat, go ahead and enjoy. And while you're enjoying, really relish it.

❋ LITTLE FREE LIBRARIES & OTHER ACTS OF LITERARY KINDNESS ❋

In 2009, Todd Bol of Hudson, Wisconsin, built a model of a one-room schoolhouse as a tribute to his mother, who was a teacher who loved to read. He filled it with books and put it on a post in his front yard. His neighbors and friends loved it, so he built several more and gave them away. Rick Brooks of the University of Wisconsin at Madison saw Bol's DIY project while they were discussing potential social enterprises. Together, the two saw a chance to achieve a variety of goals for the common good.

They were inspired by community gift-sharing networks, "take a book, leave a book" collections in coffee shops and other public spaces, and most especially by the philanthropist Andrew Carnegie. Around the beginning of the twentieth century, Carnegie set a goal of funding the creation of 2,508 free public libraries across the English-speaking world. The Wisconsin duo has gone far beyond Carnegie's goal; the number of Little Free Libraries stands at 50,000, and that number grows every day as the movement spreads from front yard to street corner to parks, walls, and storefronts, not only in all 50 states, but in over 70 countries around the world. Check out their website for more information, to sign up to receive newsletters, and/or to order a Little Free Library of your own at: https://littlefreelibrary.org/

❋ DO SOMETHING YOU LOVE ❋

What gives you great pleasure that you haven't done
in a while? Is it going to the movies and eating a large
bucket of popcorn? Reading a trashy novel? Treating
yourself to a gift? Whatever it is, give yourself
permission to indulge today.

❋ SACRED SPOT ❋

You can create an altar or other meaningful
contemplative space in just about any nook or cranny of
your house—a bookshelf, a ledge above the bathtub, a
small table in your bedroom. The point is to pick a place
where you will often go so that you can enjoy it. What
you decide to place there is of course entirely up to you.
But whatever you decide on should be something that
has meaning for you. It should not be placed on your
altar to please your Great Aunt Tilly who gave you that
hideous green statue that you really wish some child
would conveniently break.

✳ GIVE A MAY BASKET ✳

When I was a kid, we always made May baskets for all the houses in our neighborhood to celebrate May Day. We would get such a thrill out of hanging them on front doorknobs, then ringing the bell and running to a hiding spot, where we'd watch the face of the surprised recipient. May baskets are incredibly easy to make. All you need are some flowers (we always picked the first wildflowers of the season, but store-bought flowers are fine) that you've fashioned into an attractive bouquet tied with a rubber band and placed in a cone basket. To make the cone, take an 8½-by-11-inch piece of construction paper rolled into an ice-cream cone shape, with the top wider than the bottom. Staple into place and attach a paper handle (a half-inch-wide strip of construction paper) at the top with staples. Whose day can you brighten with such a gift? Your coworkers? The neighbors? Your daughter?

❋ HEALTHFUL CLEANING
PLEASURES ❋

It's time for a good spring cleaning! How about doing
it the nontoxic way? Baking soda makes an excellent
mild cleanser for kitchen and bath fixtures; just sprinkle
it straight from the box onto a damp cloth or sponge.
Use a few tablespoons dissolved in a quart of water to
wash the interiors of refrigerators and freezers; baking
soda neutralizes odors. Add a tablespoon to coffee
pots and vacuum bottles, then fill them with water and
shake to freshen them. Still on supermarket shelves, the
venerable Bon Ami cleanser is slightly more effective as
a cleaner than baking soda and doesn't contain chlorine,
phosphates, perfumes, or harsh abrasives. Baking
soda with lemon juice will remove soap film in the
bathtub and shower. Adding a few teaspoons of vinegar
to a quart of water produces a handy glass cleaner,
and equal parts of borax and washing soda (sodium
carbonate, often labeled as "detergent booster") make
an even less pungent solution for the dishwasher—a
real, all-natural replacement for overpriced dishwasher
detergent. For discolored copper pots, try an early-
twentieth-century cleanser: a tablespoon of salt mixed
with a half cup of vinegar.

❋ BLOW BUBBLES ❋

This pleasure requires a bit of money—a dollar! Buy an eight-ounce bottle of bubbles, find a small child or receptive adult and a good spot outside, and let yourself go. I guarantee you'll have a good time. Watch how the wind carries the bubbles hither and yon. Blow a few to the other person and see if she can catch them. Allow yourself the indulgence of being two years old again, if only for fifteen minutes.

❋ INDULGE IN
CREATURE COMFORTS ❋

Why do we deny ourselves so many creature comforts? I never buy the peach tea I love because it costs slightly more than regular tea. I can afford it, but I feel guilty indulging myself. How silly—my happiness is worth one dollar more a week! Wear that special pair of earrings, your favorite shirt, the perfume you save for special occasions. Today's special occasion is your own pleasure.

✳ PERSONALIZED COOKBOOKS ✳

I try to give something meaningful as gifts to those
I love, and I recently hit on a great idea. It all started
when I began to paste recipes I clipped from magazines
and newspapers into a blank book. Soon, I had almost
filled two books and friends were asking me for a
copy of this or that recipe. One friend asked me for so
many recipes I decided to make her a cookbook for her
fiftieth birthday.

I bought a beautiful blank book and divided it into
sections with little tabs—appetizers, soups and salads,
entrees, side dishes, and desserts. I then made chapter
headings for each section, photocopied all the recipes
she'd asked for or ones for dishes she had liked at my
house, and presented the book to her. She was thrilled.

That was the end of that—or so I thought. But when my college-aged daughter started complaining that she wanted a cookbook of easy gourmet dishes for students, I knew I had to spring into action again. I hope she gets as much pleasure out of receiving it as I have been getting out of figuring out what to include.

❋ LOVE DARTS ❋

My friend Sue Patton Thoele invented Love Darts: silent blessings we send to people who are driving us crazy in some way. Rather than cursing the person silently or vociferously, Sue sends a good wish—"may you be happy," for example—which if nothing else, reminds her to keep her heart open. "My favorite target," she says, "is a surly checkout person at the grocery store. I don't know how he feels about being pricked by a love dart, but I certainly feel better after sending one than I do if I grouse to myself about how rude he is." Increase your pleasure by sending love darts to anyone who annoys or frustrates you.

❋ CHANGE YOUR HAIRSTYLE ❋

This is a tried-and-true simple pleasure. When feeling down, change the style or color of your hair. It really works—particularly if you end up with a great new look. I recently changed my hairstyle after having kept it the same for a few years, and everyone I came across in the next few months told me how great I looked. I should have done it sooner!

❋ HUG SOMEONE TODAY ❋

As with so many other positive acts, it turns out that hugging boosts our immune systems. Plus it just plain feels good! So hug someone today, perhaps a person who seems particularly in need.

CHAPTER FIVE

-

SPEND TIME WITH LOVED ONES

✽ PERSONALIZED FURNITURE ✽

You can create customized furniture that you and your kids will love. Find an old chest of drawers, a wooden trunk, or other wooden furniture at a garage sale. Paint it white or another solid color. Then dip baby's hands and feet (older kids can do this themselves) in water-based latex pastel paints and gently stamp them on the top and sides of the dresser. You'll have a permanent reminder of their childhood that you—and they—will treasure always.

✼ THE PLEASURES OF
A GOOD BOOK ✼

Read out loud to family members. When our kids are young, most of us do this naturally. However, when children learn to read for themselves, we often give up this bonding activity. But we don't have to. No matter how old your child is, you can find something that you will both enjoy. Try it with your mate—I know a couple who read Lord of the Rings to each other, and they say that reading it together was much more fun than reading it on their own. Some people like reading aloud best, while others prefer being read to; find the combination that works for you.

✼ MEANINGFUL WALLPAPER ✼

I read of a wonderful idea in *365 Days of Creative Play* by Sheila Ellison and Judith Gray. Just ask your child to draw pictures of the meaningful things in his or her life, like their hopes and dreams, beliefs, and loved ones. Then make a border at the top of your child's room with the pictures. It's a great way for a kid to decorate his or her own bedroom—and what a delight for you to look at.

❋ HOLD A COOKING PARTY ❋

I love to gather a group of people to make something best made in an assembly line—cookies or tamales, for example. I buy all the ingredients, invite over neighbors or friends, open a bottle of wine, and cook, cook, cook. The time speeds by, the work goes quickly, and everyone goes home with a big pile of whatever we've made that afternoon. As far as I am concerned, a cooking party is the perfect blend of conviviality and cuisine.

❋ LOVE CLOTH ❋

For her son's first birthday, a friend of mine bought a white linen tablecloth. She has since used it only on his birthday. She invites guests at each year's birthday party to sign their names (or in the case of toddlers and very small children, to draw something, which she then signs) on his tablecloth with permanent markers. Now, ten years later, she has a colorful tablecloth full of memories that will last a lifetime. The kids love writing on it and reading all the messages from past birthdays.

✳ AROUND THE TABLE ✳

I have a strict rule which I will break only for real emergencies—that my family sits down to dinner together at the dining room table every night. I mean, if we can't eat at least one meal a day together, why do we even call ourselves a family? It's our together time, the four of us around the table telling jokes and sharing the news of our day. No TV, social media, video games, or books are allowed—just face-to-face interaction. One of the kids' favorite dinnertime conversations is what I call "remember when." Someone will start it: "Remember when I was two, Dad, and I got the flu and threw up on you?" (The grosser the better for the kids.) "Remember when you were trying to hit the golf ball in the living room and broke Mum's best plant?" The half hour or so we spend together eating, talking, and laughing is what I remember most strongly when I look back over my life.

❋ MAKE A PLAY DATE ❋

My friend Daphne and I love to play dress up. We go shopping just for fun and often don't buy a thing. We just spend a few hours trying on clothes and seeing how we look in them. Ball gowns are particularly enjoyable; just the other day we found the perfect thing for Daphne to wear to the Academy Awards if she were ever invited. She looked just like Marilyn Monroe at JFK's birthday party. How do you like to play? Do you like mountain biking? Wind surfing? Going to a spa and having a facial? Do something you think of as play today.

❋ THE PLEASURE OF GIVING PLEASURE ❋

Pleasing someone else is a pleasure like no other. Cook a special dish for your mate, find the perfect sweater for a friend, treat your child to her favorite ice cream. Today, indulge someone else in his or her simple pleasure and notice how good it makes you feel.

❋ FAMILY HOME EVENING ❋

At one point, I grew tired of running all over with all the kids every day—to soccer practice, games, piano lessons, tennis, play dates with friends—the list went on and on. I was exhausted, and the kids seemed cranky; there was never any downtime. It seemed as if we never had an evening to spend together as a family. Then I read about the tradition that Mormons have of a weekly "family home evening" and decided that was just what our family needed. And so I decreed Wednesdays would be our home evening. After dinner, all of us spend the evening together with the TV off and with no outsiders, meetings, classes, or other commitments. Sometimes we play cards or a board game, read a story aloud, or tell ghost stories; other times we bake cookies together or just read in the same room. The kids protested at first, but now they too have gotten into the spirit.

❋ PERSONALIZED
WRAPPING PAPER ❋

You and your family can make your own wrapping paper. Buy a roll of white butcher paper or brown paper. For ease, you can purchase a few rubber stamps and different colored ink pads and simply stamp out a pattern on your paper. Be careful not to smear the ink as you go—it will need a few minutes to dry. To make the paper even more personalized, you can make your own rubber stamps. Cut a potato in half, carve a simple shape into the center, then cut the sides away so your center design is elevated enough to make a clear impression. Try simple shapes like hearts, stars, dots, and diamonds. For simple polka dots, you can use wine corks. What's great about DIY giftwrap is that everyone gets to express his or her individuality.

❋ FUN WITH FICTIONARY ❋

I generally hate playing games, but recently I was introduced to one that I think is actually fun: fictionary. All you need is a few people and a dictionary. One person starts by opening the dictionary and picking a word that no one knows. Everyone writes down a made-up definition; while they are making them up, the dictionary holder writes down the correct definition. Then the dictionary holder collects all definitions and reads them aloud, and everyone votes for the correct one. If someone guesses correctly, he or she gets three points. If no one guesses the correct one, the dictionary holder gets three points. If your wrong definition is chosen, you get one point. Then the dictionary is passed to the next person. The definitions are often quite hilarious; this game offers a chance to be very creative. I once played with friends who made up such believable definitions that I was fooled again and again. I haven't laughed so hard in years.

❀ BEADING TOGETHER ❀

One great thing to do with kids is to buy an assortment of inexpensive beads (bead and craft stores abound these days) and host a beading party. If you have very young children, you can use dry macaroni (instead of beads that can too easily be popped into mouths and swallowed) that they can decorate with paint or glitter. You can then help kids string them onto elastic for

easy bracelets and necklaces. For older beaders, buy
bead thread, beading needles, and clasps to finish off
their creations.

❃ DECORATIVE
LIGHT SWITCHES ❃

One great activity that families can do together is to
decorate the light switch plates in various rooms of the
house. All you need is acrylic paints and small brushes.
Take the switch plate off the wall and paint the design
of your choice (mistakes wipe off easily with water). Let
dry thoroughly and rescrew into the wall.

❃ SOAP CARVINGS ❃

You and your kids can have fun making soap carvings
both as presents and for use at home. Just start with a
big cake of soap, a potato peeler, a butter knife, and a
nail. Use the peeler to carve a design into the soap, the
knife to cut off large areas, and the nail to draw designs.

❋ ARTISTIC HONOR ❋

Next time you host a party, create a piece of art for the guest of honor. Buy a simple canvas. Divide it into even sections using a pencil and ruler. Go over your pencil lines with permanent colored markers or paint. Provide guests with paints and brushes, and have each person decorate a square. Your honored guest will have a colorful memento of the occasion. This project works well for a variety of occasions: baby showers, housewarmings, high-school graduations, bon voyage parties, and so on.

❋ GIVE YOURSELF A NIGHT OUT ❋

My husband gets together with a group of five other guys once a month to play poker. These guys have been playing together for fifteen years. They take turns making dinner and hosting the event, and my husband never makes it home before two o'clock in the morning. I used to turn my nose up at these nights out, but I've come to see that they provide a chance for the friends not only to have fun but to keep connected to one another. They've been there for each other's marriages, births, work changes, breakups, and so on. But the main point is to have fun, and what's wrong with that? Sometimes we all need to go out, stay up late, and kick up our heels. When was the last time you did something like this?

❋ OLD-FASHIONED GAMES ❋

When the kids have been cooped up in the house too long playing Nintendo and watching TV and have steam to let off, why not suggest that they round up the neighbor kids and try out some of the games that were popular in previous generations? You'll recognize them: leapfrog, hopscotch, king of the hill, duck duck goose, red light, Mother may I, Simon says, marbles, and jacks. Who says fun has to come in a box and cost fifty dollars or more? Maybe they will even entice you to join them in a trip down memory lane.

❋ CELEBRATE THE SOLSTICE ❋

I love the sun, and so it is natural for me to celebrate the summer solstice, the longest day of the year, with a barbecue bash on my deck for all my friends. Having asked everyone to bring their own food to barbecue, I always serve sangria to the adults and lemonade to the kids, make a big vat of potato salad, and voilà: instant celebration. We feast and laugh—kids and grownups alike—play silly games like red rover and blindman's buff, and we have a grand old time enjoying the first day of summer.

✳ FAMILY SLUMBER PARTY ✳

When my in-laws are visiting, we sometimes prepare
a late-night snack (such as ice cream with fruit sauce),
change into pajamas, open the futon in the family room,
bring plenty of extra blankets and cushions, spread out
on sofas and mattresses, and tell stories. We stay up
late, then fall asleep all together. It is then that I feel
most like a part of their big, warmhearted family.

✳ ALL YOU CAN EAT ✳

I have a friend whose family has an annual ice cream
dinner one day each summer. They walk to the corner
ice cream parlor and each order a single cone, any flavor
they want. They then walk around, eating, until they're
finished. Then they return to the store and repeat the
process until they're completely satisfied. (My friend
remembers that when he turned fourteen, his record
was six cones—all strawberry.)

❀ PLAYING FUN ❀

My group of friends always holds an annual board game tournament sometime in the fall. We arrive early, around five o'clock, game boards in hand, have a potluck supper, and then get down to playing. The more the merrier, because then there can be a game of Risk going on in one room while Pictionary is being played in another and a game of Dictionary in yet another. People decide what they want to play, and as their game finishes, they roam around looking to join another group or to start a new game. The gaming continues until the wee hours of the morning.

❀ NIGHT AT THE (HOME) MOVIES ❀

Host a movie party at home for your family. Agree on movies that everyone would like to watch, make plenty of popcorn, and offer a variety of drinks and candy treats.

CHAPTER SIX

–

ENHANCING THE SENSES

❋ THE NOSE KNOWS ❋

What can compare to the smell of home cooking as you walk in the door after a hard day's work? I like it so much that I've taken to Crock-Pot cooking on my nights to cook so that the aromas will be awaiting me as soon as I hit the kitchen doorway. There's nothing like a Crock-Pot meal!

❋ DON'T FORGET THE DIMMER ❋

Why is that when people are installing dimmers, they always remember the bedroom, dining room, and living room but ignore the kitchen? Whenever I move into a new house, putting a dimmer in the kitchen is my priority. That way, when guests come over and gather in the kitchen, as they invariably will, the lighting is as soft and flattering as it is in the rest of the house.

❋ SCENTED CANDLES ❋

Surprise your sweetheart with a candlelit dinner for
two graced by your own homemade scented candles
both on the table and in the bedroom. Their lovely
fragrance will be released as they burn. Scented candles
are incredibly easy to make—you just need to plan in
advance. (If you haven't planned ahead, you can still get
some of the effect by sprinkling a drop or two of your
favorite essential oil in the melted wax of a plain candle
as it burns.)

- 2 OUNCES OF YOUR FAVORITE FRAGRANCE
  ESSENTIAL OIL (OR TRY A COMBINATION;
  VANILLA AND ROSE ARE MY FAVORITES
  FOR ROMANCE)
- ¼ CUP ORRIS ROOT POWDER (AVAILABLE
  AT HERBAL STORES, AND IT CAN BE
  ORDERED ONLINE)
- 1 LARGE AIRTIGHT PLASTIC CONTAINER BIG
  ENOUGH TO HOLD 6 CANDLES
- 6 UNSCENTED CANDLES, ANY SIZE

Combine the oil(s) and the orris root and sprinkle in the
bottom of the container. Place candles inside, cover,
and store in a cool spot for 4 to 6 weeks.

❋ FACIAL SAUNA ❋

- 2 DROPS FENNEL ESSENTIAL OIL
- 2 DROPS LAVENDER ESSENTIAL OIL
- 2 DROPS LEMON ESSENTIAL OIL
- 2 DROPS ORANGE ESSENTIAL OIL

Mix oils together and pour into a bowl of steaming water. Drape a towel over your head and the bowl and sit, allowing the steam to penetrate your pores. Be careful not to put your face too close—this should be luxurious, not a painful experience!

❃ ALL-PURPOSE ROOM SPRAY ❃

When the house feels musty and stale, try this aromatherapy spray to freshen things up a bit. The authors of *Seasons of Aromatherapy* also recommend adding a few drops of it to your laundry to freshen up the clean clothes.

- 4 DROPS LAVENDER ESSENTIAL OIL
- 2 DROPS PEPPERMINT ESSENTIAL OIL
- 2 DROPS TEA TREE ESSENTIAL OIL
- 2 CUPS WATER

Combine all ingredients in a spray bottle. Spray your rooms.

❃ INSTANT GOURMET ❃

You can easily make your own infused olive oils. Buy some decorative bottles or use recycled wine bottles. Be sure to use only fresh herbs and wash them well. Also make sure the oil completely covers all the ingredients, and then seal the bottle tightly and use within three weeks. Because fresh garlic contains the spores for a microbe that, when added to oil, can cause botulism, it's best not to make any garlic-flavored oil at home (the store-bought kind uses sterilized garlic). To make chili oil, simply add 5 yellow Thai chilies and 1 teaspoon peppercorns to 5 cups of olive oil, cap the bottle tightly, and let stand in a cool place for a week. For lemon pepper oil, first slice a lemon for each bottle you plan to make and dry lemon slices in the oven at 170°F for about 5 hours, or until dry but not crisp. To a 5-cup bottle of oil, add 1 tablespoon whole black peppercorns and the slices from one dried lemon. For rosemary oil, add 3 large sprigs of rosemary to a 5-cup bottle of olive oil.

❊ INDULGE IN DINNER ❊

It's easy to get the winter blues. I remember when I lived in Ithaca, New York, it could be overcast for six weeks or more at a time during the winter. By March each year, I was really down. So, to combat the winter blues, take the opportunity tonight to indulge yourself with a really good dinner. Make your favorite food. Buy fresh flowers, use cloth napkins, light a scented candle. Go all out for no other reason than to enjoy yourself.

❊ USE GOOD SCENTS ❊

Smells can be mood elevators. Here are some ways to
bring good scents into your day. Light a candle with a
favorite scent before you go to bed, letting it perfume
the room. My favorite is Casablanca lily. Jasmine is
a good choice too; it induces optimism. Just be sure
to blow out the candle before you fall asleep. Apply
a scented lotion or one or two drops of your favorite
essential oil to your temples and rub gently. Various
body stores even have specialized "pulse point" lotions.

❋ MINTCENSE ❋

Originally made in colonial times, when it was believed to "clear the head," mint potpourri makes an excellent natural room freshener. The following was taken from a recipe by Phyllis Shaudys, who says the concoction sells well at craft fairs.

- ½ CUP ORRIS ROOT
- ½ TABLESPOON OIL OF LAVENDER OR PENNYROYAL
- 2 CUPS DRIED ORANGE MINT
- 2 CUPS DRIED SPEARMINT
- 2 CUPS DRIED PEPPERMINT
- 1 CUP DRIED THYME
- 1 CUP DRIED ROSEMARY

Combine the orris root and essential oil. Add the rest of the ingredients and combine gently, taking care not to crush the leaves too much. Store in a covered jar. To use, shake and then open the jar, allowing the potpourri's aroma to scent the space.

✳ AROMATIC TRIVET ✳

This kitchen delight will release a fabulous fragrance every time you place a hot pan on it. These trivets are so simple to make, you should consider making some for yourself and for your friends.

- 20 INCHES STURDY FABRIC, SUCH AS MATTRESS TICKING
- SCISSORS
- NEEDLE AND THREAD
- STUFFING: BROKEN CINNAMON STICKS, CLOVES, AND BAY LEAVES
- UPHOLSTERY NEEDLE
- COTTON STRING

Cut two twenty to twenty-five inch pieces of fabric and place right sides together, i.e., inside out from how they will end up. Pin and stitch the pieces together, leaving an opening large enough for the stuffing to fit through. Trim the seams and turn right side out. Fill with stuffing material and then slip-stitch the opening using the upholstery needle threaded with string. Make four separate stitches in the center of the pad, forming a square, clearing the contents away from the stitch. Finish each with a simple knot. Makes 1 trivet.

✳ HOMEMADE VANILLA EXTRACT ✳

Yes, you can make it yourself, and it is unbelievably easy. If you place the extract in a pretty glass bottle, it makes a lovely little gift.

- 1 VANILLA BEAN
- 1 FOUR-OUNCE BOTTLE WITH TOP
- SCANT 4 OUNCES UNFLAVORED VODKA

Split the bean in half, put it in the bottle, and pour in the vodka. Cap and let sit at least one month (the longer, the stronger the vanilla flavor).

✳ TAKE A DIP IN THE OCEAN-AT HOME ✳

Have you ever noticed how great you feel after a swim in the ocean? Part of the reason is that the magnesium, zinc, and potassium in sea salt draw out the lactic acid from your muscles, easing tension. You can simulate the effect in a luxurious bath. Pour one cup of salt into the stream of warm water while filling the tub, turn on

an ocean CD or tape, light a sea breeze-scented candle,
and indulge.

❋ GARLIC SOUP ❋

Cultures throughout the world swear by garlic soup as
a spring tonic and all-around cure for that under-the-
weather feeling. Don't let the huge quantity of garlic
scare you off—when cooked, it becomes very mellow.

- 4 HEADS OF GARLIC
- 1 BUNCH PARSLEY, THYME, AND/OR
  MARJORAM, TIED INTO A BUNDLE WITH STRING
- 1 QUART CHICKEN BROTH, VEGETABLE
  BROTH, OR WATER
- JUICE OF 1 LEMON OR LIME
- SALT AND PEPPER TO TASTE
- OPTIONAL: LIGHTLY TOASTED BREAD
  OR CROUTONS

Break up the heads of garlic into cloves, discarding the
papery outer membrane, but don't peel the cloves. Place
garlic cloves in a 4-quart soup pot with the herbs. Add
the broth or water, cover, and bring to a boil. Lower the

heat and simmer for about 30 minutes, until garlic is very soft. Strain the soup through the fine disk of a food mill or, in the alternative, puree in a blender or food processor, then push through a medium-mesh strainer with the back of a ladle. Add the lemon or lime juice, salt and pepper, and bread or croutons, if desired. Serves 4.

❋ ROOM REFRESHER ❋

If you use a room deodorizer, you don't need to throw it away as the scent begins to wane. Simply put a few drops of your favorite perfume on top of it, and it will continue to scent the air.

❋ ROSE POTPOURRI ❋

This is a real treat for rose lovers.

- ½ TEASPOON ROSE ESSENTIAL OIL
- 1½ TABLESPOONS ORRIS ROOT
- 2 CUPS DRIED ROSE PETALS
- 2 CUPS DRIED ROSE GERANIUM LEAVES

Combine the oil and orris root and let the mixture sit for a few days. Add to the flowers and leaves and stir well. Keep it in a covered container until ready to use. Makes 4 cups.

❋ HOMEMADE INFUSED VINEGARS ❋

Before the herbs in your garden die back, why not use them in homemade vinegars? Packaged in pretty bottles, these infused vinegars make a unique gift. Pick and wash the herbs to be used: long sprigs of basil, rosemary, thyme, sage, or a combination all work well and look beautiful in the bottles. Dried herbs will not work as well. The rule of thumb is 1 cup of fresh herbs per quart of vinegar. Dry the fresh herbs well by laying them on paper towels for a few minutes. Pack them into clean bottles or jars with lids or corks, then fill each with white wine vinegar that has been heated to a pre-boil. Cork or cap. Stand the jars on a sunny windowsill for about two weeks (or four weeks if not very sunny). The warmth of the sun will infuse the vinegar with the herbs. Taste test; if it doesn't seem flavorful enough, strain the vinegar and add more herbs.

Label and decorate the jars with a beautiful ribbon and store at room temperature. For a more lively infusion, try chili garlic vinegar: add as many dried whole red chilies as will fit in your bottle, a tablespoon of slightly crushed whole peppercorns, and five slightly crushed garlic cloves.

❁ SCENTED ORNAMENTS ❁

Here's another wonderful and simple decorating idea. No, the ornaments are not edible!

- 1 FOUR-OUNCE CAN GROUND CINNAMON (ABOUT 1 CUP)
- 1 TABLESPOON GROUND CLOVES
- 1 TABLESPOON GROUND NUTMEG
- ¾ CUP APPLESAUCE
- 2 TABLESPOONS WHITE GLUE
- OPTIONAL: THREAD, GLITTER GLUE, FABRIC, OR OTHER DECORATING ITEMS

In a medium bowl, combine cinnamon, cloves, and nutmeg. Add applesauce and glue; stir to combine. Work mixture with hands 2 to 3 minutes or until dough is smooth and ingredients are thoroughly mixed. Divide dough into 4 portions. Roll out each dough portion to quarter-inch thickness. Cut dough with cookie cutters. Using a toothpick, make a small hole through the top of each ornament. Place cut-out ornaments on wire rack to dry. Allow several days to dry, turning ornaments over once a day. Create hanger loops by pushing a length of thread through the hole at the top of each one. Decorate as desired with glitter, beads, or fabric.

❋ CELEBRATE LIGHT ❋

On solstice night (December twenty-first), gather candles and matches and then turn off all the lights in your home. After dwelling on the dark for a few moments, light the candles and welcome the light back into the world.

CHAPTER SEVEN

-

MAKING TIME
FOR REST

✳ FEAST OF WORDS ✳

My idea of a good time these days is to stay in bed as long as possible in the morning reading a good book. Between working and parenting, I can never get enough of it. Sometimes I even wake up in the middle of the night and read for a couple hours just to get my fix. For my birthday, my husband entertained our daughter all day so that I could stay in bed with a thick thriller. What fun!

❋ HOPS FOR A
GREAT NIGHT'S SLEEP ❋

The herb hops is said to be mildly sleep inducing, while lavender induces a sense of well-being. Together they make a great filling for a sleep pillow.

- 1 TEN-BY-EIGHT-INCH PIECE OF MUSLIN
- 4 HANDFULS DRIED HOP FLOWERS
- 2 HANDFULS DRIED LAVENDER

Sew up three sides of the muslin and add the hops and lavender. Slip-stitch the open end to close up the pillow. Pillow should be relatively flat. Tuck it under your cheek when you go to bed to bring relaxation and deepened rest. Makes 1 pillow.

❋ THE COMFY COUCH ❋

What greater pleasure does life have to offer than a mid-afternoon Saturday nap on a comfy couch? Treat yourself to that delicious feeling you get when you know you should be up doing chores but instead are stretched out, luxuriating in doing absolutely nothing.

✻ GOOD FOR WHAT
AILS YOU ✻

If you suffer from menstrual cramps or premenstrual discomfort, you may find the following bath remedy to be soothing and calming. The water will dilate your blood vessels and relax your muscles, while the herbs provide aromatherapy.

- 2 TABLESPOONS DRIED LAVENDER
- 2 TABLESPOONS DRIED ROSE PETALS
- 3 TABLESPOONS DRIED CHAMOMILE
- 2 TABLESPOONS HOPS

Combine the herbs in a glass or ceramic bowl and pour in a quart of boiling water. Cover and let sit for an hour. Strain the herbs and pour the aromatic infusion into your tub under the running tap of a warm (not hot) bath.

✻ FREE VACATION ✻

When my husband is away, I sometimes spend the night in the guest bedroom in the old-fashioned double bed I used before I was married. It has a fluffy comforter, ruffled pillow shams, and pretty sheets. If I adjust the miniblinds just right, I get a lovely view of the treetops and city lights, a nice contrast to the tar-and-gravel rooftops and power lines I see during the day. And because there is only one outlet in the room, just enough for a lamp and a clock, I read in bed instead of watching TV. Spending the night in the guest room makes me feel as though I'm staying at a bed and breakfast. As Jane Austen once said, "There is nothing like staying at home for real comfort."

❋ DEEP BREATH ❋

If you run yourself ragged rushing through the day and seem not to be able to find a time to slow down, take a tip from Vietnamese Buddhist monk Thich Nhat Hanh, who recommends that each time the telephone rings, you notice three breaths before you answer. He suggests it as a way to become aware of the present moment, but it is also fabulous for coming back into your body and reducing tension. The more the phone rings, the more relaxed and present you will be!

❋ GET A MAKEOVER ❋

This is another feel-good, absolutely free simple pleasure. Just go to any large department store and cruise the makeup counters. Choose someone to make you over. Perhaps you'll end up liking how you look so much that you buy some skin and beauty products. But you can have fun playing whether or not you buy anything. (I also love to go to the wig section and see how I'd look in various hair colors and styles; I make a hideous blonde!)

❋ SOUND SLEEP SUGGESTIONS ❋

Doesn't getting lots of sleep feel great? Experts say we are a sleep-deprived nation and that we need between seven and eight hours of sleep a night, no matter how absorbed we are in that new novel or late-night talk show. Shorten sleeping time, and we lose that most valuable period just before we awaken, when our bodies recharge to deal with stress.

Here's some common advice: Get to bed a half hour earlier than usual and, after a few weeks, add another half hour. Ease toward bedtime with quiet activities such as reading, stretching, and meditation. Don't drink caffeine in the evening, and don't smoke or drink alcohol before bedtime. To deal with continual insomnia, one study by a clinical psychologist has come up with dramatically reverse advice: Spend less time in bed to cut down on the frustration of lying awake. Forced to stay awake until, say, one o'clock in the morning, insomniacs drop off to sleep more easily. When they were able to sleep soundly during those limited hours, they gradually extended their time in bed. One more intriguing idea—use the bedroom exclusively for sleep and sex.

✳ LAVENDER BATH OIL ✳

Here's another great way to relax.

- 1 CUP ALMOND OR GRAPESEED OIL
- ½ TEASPOON LAVENDER ESSENTIAL OIL
- ¼ TEASPOON VITAMIN E OIL
- DRIED LAVENDER SPRIGS
- 10-OUNCE DECORATIVE BOTTLE WITH A TOP RIBBON AND GIFT TAG, IF DESIRED

Combine the essential oil and vitamin E oil in a glass container and then test the scent on your skin. (You might want to add a bit more of one thing or another depending on the resulting fragrance.) Place the lavender sprigs into the bottle. Using a funnel, pour the almond or grapeseed oil into the bottle and close the top. Store in a cool, dry place.

✽ BODY BREAK ✽

Just for today, stop thinking of your body as something that must be whipped into shape and notice what would give it pleasure. What would your body like? To lie down? To go for a leisurely walk? To make love? Sometimes just giving yourself permission to notice what you really desire can be an amazing way to find happiness—or at least peace of mind.

✽ SEVEN-PILLOW ROYALTY DAY ✽

On the seven-pillow royalty day, you stay in bed all day (if that appeals to you). It takes a bit of preparation, not only to find the time to goof off but also to stock up on the supplies you'll need: the books you've been longing to read, the exact food you want to eat in bed, a journal to write or draw in, polish to paint your nails, favorite movies, and plenty of bolsters and pillows on which to luxuriate. The point is to have a totally self-indulgent, lying around kind of day in which you stay in bed as long as you want, doing exactly what you want, eating only what you want. It's a great antidote to too much running around and attending to other people's needs. Instead, you pretend you're royalty and cater to your every whim. If you've got kids or a spouse, schedule one royalty day for each of you on different weekends and take turns being the babysitter. Believe me, it will do your heart, mind, and body good!

❋ HEADACHE RUB ❋

Here's an old-fashioned German cure for headaches.

- 1 QUART WHITE ROSE PETALS
- 1 QUART JAR, STERILIZED
- ABOUT 1 QUART 90-PROOF VODKA (OR SUBSTITUTE RUBBING ALCOHOL)

Pack the jar with the rose petals. Pour the vodka over the petals and let stand, covered, for at least 24 hours. Rub mixture on forehead, temples, and back of neck.

❊ PERCHANCE TO DREAM ❊

Are you having trouble falling asleep? Consider this natural aromatherapy remedy—a sleep potion made with, among other oils, lavender. Lavender is an adaptogen, which means that it can be stimulating or relaxing, depending on your energy needs. If you are tired, it will help you fall asleep.

In a small plastic spray bottle, combine 4 drops lavender essential oil, 3 drops orange essential oil, and 3 drops chamomile essential oil (another good sleep aid), together with 5 ounces of water. Shake well. Spray sheets, pillowcases, and the air in the bedroom before bed.

❊ HERBAL BATHS ❊

Many stores offer wonderful "tub teas," collections of herbs packed in oversized tea bags to drop in the bathtub while it fills. If you are feeling ambitious, you can even make your own. Simply use thread or string to tie a few bags of an herbal tea you like to the tap. You can also fill a tea infusion ball with herbs or tie up herbs in a double thickness of cheesecloth. You can even use the foot of a clean nylon stocking. Afterward, you can let the bag dry (be careful where it drips) and use it for a few more baths. Alternatively, pour a pint of boiling water over dried or fresh herbs, steep covered for 10 minutes, then strain into the tub. A variety of herbs are available at stores specializing in natural foods and remedies. Here are some traditional combinations: For a relaxing bath, combine chamomile, jasmine, and hops. For a stimulating bath, use marigold, lavender, bay, mint, rosemary, and thyme. For a healing bath, try calendula, comfrey, and spearmint.

❋ SIMPLE POST-WORK PAMPERING ❋

There are many ways to pamper yourself when you get home from work. One very simple one is to change out of work clothes and anoint yourself with an essential oil. One of our favorites is a combination we call "vamber." Pour equal parts of amber and vanilla essential oils into a vial. Shake well. The result is a uniquely rich and sensual combination that is both comforting and sexy—perfect for the evening.

❀ HERBAL BATH
COLD REMEDY ❀

When you start having the sniffles, try this soothing bath.

- 2 TABLESPOONS DRIED EUCALYPTUS
- 4 TABLESPOONS DRIED ROSEMARY
- 4 TABLESPOONS DRIED LAVENDER BUDS
- 2 TABLESPOONS DRIED ROSEBUDS

Steep the above ingredients in boiling water for 30 minutes. Strain and add the remaining liquid to a warm (not hot) bath.

❀ DECLARE A
WATCHLESS DAY ❀

Set aside a totally unscheduled day, with nothing to do and no one to attend to. Take off your watch. Then follow your own rhythm throughout the day, doing exactly what you want, when you want.

❋ GO OUT ON A DATE WITH YOURSELF ❋

What do you love to do that you haven't done in a long time? Riding horseback? Going to a concert? Getting a massage? Make a date with yourself to do it.

❋ TAKING THE WATERS ❋

For a relaxing bath, add lavender or chamomile oil to running water. Start with ¼ teaspoon for a whole tub of water. For scents to inspire your sensuality, try ¼ teaspoon of sandalwood, ylang–ylang, or cinnamon essential oils. These can be blended in various combinations—experiment to find out what works best for you.

For an invigorating bath, try clipping a few pieces of fresh rosemary from your garden (or buy them at the grocery store in the fresh produce section). Take a piece of cheesecloth, tulle, or fine netting and tie the rosemary up in it with a piece of twine or thread. Pound it with a mallet to release its aromatic oils. Hold the sachet under warm running water, then let it float in the bath.

✿ LOVE BATH ✿

So named because I love to use this herbal combination.

- 1 CUP DRIED LAVENDER
- 1 CUP DRIED ROSEMARY
- 1 CUP DRIED ROSE PETALS
- ½ CUP DRIED LOVAGE
- ½ CUP DRIED LEMON VERBENA
- ¼ CUP EACH DRIED THYME, MINT, SAGE, AND ORRIS ROOT
- MUSLIN

Mix all dried herbs together and store in a covered container. When you want to take a bath, place ¼ cup of herbal mix in the center of an eight-inch square of muslin and tie tightly with a piece of string. Boil this ball in 1 quart of water for 10 minutes. Draw a warm bath, pour in the herbal water, and then use the ball to scrub your body. Makes 16 bath balls.

CHAPTER EIGHT

-

REFLECTING ON LIFE

✳ TIME CAPSULE ✳

A family I know recently made a family time capsule, and all three kids—ages five, seven, and twelve—really enjoyed it. They took an old trunk, and each person put in something to represent themselves, something they considered important. They put in the day's newspaper, a grocery store receipt (it was the twelve-year-old's idea to compare prices now and then), and photos of themselves they had recently taken. Then they sealed it and put a note on top saying they would open it in 2035. They all had a great time together deciding what to include.

✳ APRIL SHOWERS ✳

My favorite household chore is giving my indoor plants their yearly spring shower. I carry them all outside and thoroughly hose them off with water, sometimes hand washing individual leaves if they are particularly dusty. Then I pluck dead leaves and bulbs, trim brown ends with scissors, and replace old soil with fresh if needed. When I return the plants indoors, they sparkle so much I could swear they were thanking me.

❋ BUTTERFLY HAVEN ❋

If you want to increase the butterfly population in
your yard this summer, you can plant a wide variety
of flowers to attract them, including common yarrow,
New York aster, Shasta daisy, coreopsis, horsemint,
lavender, rosemary, thyme, butterfly bush, shrubby
cinquefoil, common garden petunia, verbena,
pincushion flowers, cosmos, zinnia, globe amaranth,
purple coneflower, sunflowers, lupine, and delphinium.
Keep in mind that butterflies also need wind protection,
a quiet place to lay eggs, and access to drinking water.

❋ MAKE A MEMORY BOX ❋

Find or buy a box you like and put your favorite things
in it. Choose things that feel good because they bring
back good memories—the picture of your newborn (he's
now twenty-seven), the single remaining earring from
the pair your husband bought you while he was on a
business trip as a surprise present, the flowers from
the day he told you he loved you. As the memories flood
back, you will instantly feel happy.

✳ MORNING WONDER RITUAL ✳

The great cellist Pablo Casals once said, "For the
past eighty years, I have started each day in the same
manner. It is not a mechanical routine but something
essential to my daily life. I go to the piano and I play two
preludes and fugues of Bach. I cannot think of doing
otherwise. It is a sort of benediction on the house. But
that is not its only meaning for me. It is a rediscovery
of the world in which I have the joy of being a part. It
fills me with awareness of the wonder of life, with a
feeling of the incredible marvel of being a human being."
What small thing can you do when you wake up in the
morning to tap into that sense of marvel? Play a special
piece of music? Read something inspirational? For me,
it's cuddling in bed with my daughter, looking up at the
redwood tree framed in the skylight, and listening to all
the birds sing.

✳ WORM FARM ✳

Here's an activity to do with little ones. Search your
yard for about ten worms. Fill a gallon glass jar with
alternating layers of sand and garden soil until the jar

is almost full. Then add compost items such as coffee grounds, banana peels cut into pieces, and old dried leaves. Place the worms on the top and cover the jar with a piece of black cloth secured by a rubber band. Whenever curiosity strikes, remove the cloth for a few minutes and see what the worms are up to. When interest wanes, return the worms to the garden.

❋ KEEP MEMORIES ALIVE ❋

There are a number of wonderful ways to display photos inexpensively. Here are some ideas to get you started:

To make photo collages, collect different-sized pictures in frames from yard sales and flea markets. Take the pictures out of the frames and discard them. Cut a poster board the size of each frame for the backdrop, then create a collage with snapshots by gluing the pictures to the poster board and then inserting the poster board into the frame. Think in themes: birthdays, holidays over the years, your daughter's volleyball career, vacation shots of you and your husband— get creative.

Purchase inexpensive clear eight-by-ten-inch acrylic box frames and have favorite photos blown up to eight by ten inches. Arrange them attractively on the wall.

Find old window frames without glass. Tack pictures and other mementos on the wall and place the window frames over them to create the illusion of looking through a window.

❃ GARDEN JOURNAL ❃

Keeping a garden journal can be wonderfully satisfying. You don't have to limit yourself to the facts—your journal can also be a place to muse, collect quotes, and keep in touch with nature's wisdom. The key is to recognize that it can be a visual record as well as a written one—dry and paste the first sweet pea your son grew; photos of your orchid cactus in bloom; a smattering of fall leaves on the day you found out you were pregnant, surrounded by the poem your spouse wrote for the occasion; or a sketch of the color of the sky on a memorable winter day. Workshop leader Barry Hopkins, who calls these Earthbound Journals, suggests you start with a blank, hardcover artist sketchbook at least 7½ by 8½ inches, an Exacto knife for cutting, watercolors for borders, Cray-Pas pastels for flowers, aerosol glue for pasting, and fixative to keep pencils and pastel colors from smudging.

Make your own cover for your journal—you can use old bits of a special shirt, for example. If you have an electric drill, drill through the book to make holes on an edge and create a ribbon or rawhide fastener. Follow your own creativity where it leads you and imbue the book with memories of your garden.

* PUBLIC GARDENING *

Are you longing for a garden but have no place for one? Take advantage of the variety of places that have gardens you can visit: zoos, public parks, cemeteries, college campuses, garden club tours, nurseries and garden centers, or a friend's house. These days, you can also find community gardens and gardening coops where you can get your hands dirty. Call your parks and recreation department. (All of the above are also great places to get ideas if you do have a garden of your own.)

❋ REFLECTED GLORY ❋

Martha Stewart is renowned for making beautiful things by carrying out steps that are often complicated. However, sometimes she has an idea that is simplicity itself. One such suggestion I recently saw is to line the edges of a garden path with pure white stones, pebbles, and shells. That way, at nightfall, "They'll reflect the moonlight, showing you the way."

❋ LEGACY OF TREES ❋

Our family has decided to plant three trees, representing our three family members, in each of the fifty states. The places we're picking contain either our last name or one of our first names. We're doing it because we believe planting trees is a way to help protect nature, beautify the landscape, and provide habitat for birds and animals. So far, we've been to twenty states and have been received graciously in each town we've visited. We generally find a family that is willing to have us plant a tree in their yard, but we've also done a few street trees.

✽ PLANT SOMETHING SPECIAL ✽

My husband and I planted a hydrangea that was on the altar at our wedding. It moves with us from house to house as a symbol of our marriage. Other people plant trees to honor loved ones who have died or to commemorate a special anniversary. And many people plant birth trees for their children. You can involve your child in helping to take care of the tree and in tracking its growth by tying a bit of yarn to the outmost tip of a branch each fall and seeing where the yarn ends up after the next summer.

✽ WATCH THE SUNRISE OR SUNSET ✽

It doesn't matter which you choose, although sometimes it's more fun to pick the one you usually don't see. But this time, really watch it, not as a backdrop, but, at least for the moment, as the main event.

❋ CHILDHOOD DELIGHTS ❋

What's your favorite food memory from childhood? Mine is my grandmother's fudge and her mustard pickles (not eaten together, thank you). I haven't had either in years. Chances are you haven't recently indulged in your nursery favorites either, but maybe today is the time to splurge. Do you have the recipes? If not, can you call a relative and track them down? Chances are your Aunt Tilly's world-famous potato salad recipe was from a mayonnaise jar. My grandma's "one-of-a-kind" fudge is still printed on jars of Marshmallow Fluff.

❋ HANDMADE BANDBOXES ❋

In the Victorian era, bandboxes were smaller versions of lady's hatboxes. You can make your own very easily by keeping your eye out for interestingly shaped cardboard boxes with loose-fitting lids (so they will close when the fabric is added). But even an old shoe box will do quite nicely, as will a heart-shaped candy box.

- **1 CARDBOARD BOX WITH LOOSE–FITTING LID**
- **LIGHTWEIGHT FABRIC, WALLPAPER, OR WRAPPING PAPER OF YOUR CHOICE**
- **SPRAY GLUE FOR PAPER**
- **FABRIC GLUE FOR FABRIC**

Place paper or fabric on the top of the lid and measure to fit, leaving one inch on each side to allow for overlap. Do the same for the sides of the box. Cover the side of the box by applying a light coat of appropriate glue. Fold the excess covering material and glue to the inside and bottom of the box. Cover the top of the lid, clipping the excess paper or fabric every inch or so, and then press the extra inch tabs over onto the rim and glue. Then cut paper or fabric for the rim, taking care to match patterns and to conceal raw edges. Fold the top of the rim down and glue to the rim of the box lid. Glue the raw edges of the rim at the bottom to the inside.

✳ GIFTS OF THE SPIRIT ✳

I once came across a newsletter called *Jumpin' Jan's Flash*. The author recommended eight wonderful gifts of the spirit that can really bring happiness to you and your loved ones: the gift of listening, the gift of affection, the gift of laughter, the gift of a note of love and appreciation, the gift of a compliment, the gift of a favor, the gift of solitude, and the gift of a cheerful disposition. Consider the simple pleasure of giving of yourself.

✳ WEB TIME ✳

Take time on a damp fall morning to observe a spider while she weaves her web in the garden. Watch her as she moves inside the rim, patiently and methodically, reaching out her leg to catch a strand of silk from her own body, threading it to a spoke and moving on, repeating the motion again and again. It will make you marvel at the endless magic of nature. More importantly, twenty minutes in her company will fill you with calm.

✳ CREATE A LOVE GALLERY ✳

Years ago, my husband and I started putting pictures of loved ones up on a wall in our living room. They never failed to give me a lift as I walked in the door at the end of the day. We've moved several times, but our photo gallery always goes with us—hallways are a particularly good place for this. If you don't want to go to the trouble of framing photos (we buy inexpensive black frames that create a visual harmony), you can simply tack photos onto a bulletin board or attach them to the fridge with magnets—any place where they will bring a smile to your lips.

✳ RITUAL OF APPRECIATION ✳

You can do this anytime, anywhere, but this ritual, which I call "Appreciations," is great around the Thanksgiving table. It's wonderful for bringing people closer, even those who don't know one another very well (because you can always find something to appreciate about someone, even if it is the Brussels sprouts casserole he contributed to dinner). It's effective with alienated kids who tend to hear nothing but complaints about them most of the time.

"Appreciations" works best when everyone chooses one person as the focus and then everyone else, as the spirit moves them, speaks about that person. When everyone who wants to has spoken, move on to focus on the next person. There are four rules: remarks must be positive (no sarcasm or backhanded compliments), no one else may interject anything while someone is speaking, no one has to say anything if he or she doesn't want to speak, and the object of the appreciations, instead of responding, just silently takes in the praise. It's surprising how difficult this last rule is—but you'll get used to it!

❋ EXPERIENCING GREAT HOLIDAYS ❋

When you think of the six-week period between Thanksgiving and the first of the year, do you look forward to the time with eager anticipation or a sense of dread? For so many of us, the holidays, which should be filled with opportunities for pleasure—a sense of togetherness, a chance to give, a chance to be grateful— are instead occasions for fights, disappointment, overspending, and fatigue.

Today, just take a moment to figure out why the holidays are not pleasurable for you. Do you or those around you have unrealistic expectations that you run around trying to fulfill? Do you overspend? Do the holidays bring up feelings of loneliness? Do you have trouble getting along with the relatives that you will spend time with? Today all you have to do is to identify where the holidays get derailed for you and to make a commitment to finding ways to increase your holiday pleasure.

CHAPTER NINE

-

ACTS OF KINDNESS

❋ BASKET OF LOVE ❋

Do you want to surprise your paramour some evening?
Make a love basket. Simply find a heart–shaped basket,
spray–paint it red (sand it slightly first so the paint will
stick better), add a pretty ribbon to the handle, and then
fill it with your beloved's favorite things: chocolate-
covered cherries, sexy underwear—whatever your
sweetheart fancies. Then place it on your love's pillow
to be discovered.

❋ HEARTFELT VALENTINE'S DAY ❋

This year, rather than buying a card, why not make your loved ones personalized Valentine's Day cards? All you and/or your kids really need is imagination—it's totally possible to make a Valentine that the recipient will never forget. To get started, consider the following:

- LOOK THROUGH A BOOK OF POETRY TO FIND JUST THE RIGHT VERSE.
- BE BRAVE AND TRY EXPRESSING YOUR THOUGHTS DIRECTLY.
- TAKE AN 8½–BY–11–INCH PIECE OF CONSTRUCTION PAPER AND FOLD IN HALF. KEEPING A QUARTER–INCH MARGIN AT TOP AND BOTTOM OF FOLD AND BETWEEN EACH DESIGN, CUT LITTLE HALF–HEARTS AND OTHER DESIGNS IN THE FOLD. OPEN IT UP AND VOILÀ! YOU'VE CREATED A HOMEMADE LACE BORDER.
- DECORATE WITH LACE DOILIES, GLITTER, DRIED FLOWERS, AND BITS OF RIBBON.

✸ LATE-NIGHT LOVE NOTES ✸

Last Valentine's Day, I started a new tradition with my husband. I gave him a little journal that was only to be used for writing love notes to each other. We keep it in the bedside table drawer, and whenever we feel compelled, we make an entry and then hide it under the other person's pillow. There's nothing like getting into bed, feeling that little lump under your head, and realizing that you have sweet words from your beloved to read before going to sleep.

✸ SETTING THE SCENE ✸

If you want great sex, think about creating a bedroom that's conducive to intimacy, says Will Ross in *The Wonderful Little Sex Book*. "It doesn't need to be elaborately furnished, but it should be uncluttered, have pleasing colors, and not be merely utilitarian; it should inspire a sense of beauty. The bed you use for sex ought to have a special, exotic, otherworldly feeling, almost evocative of an altar. There should be an air of reverence. Some people enjoy making love under a canopy, and you may want to construct one. Soft lighting is immensely helpful, and so is quietly pulsating music. When the whole room feels like a retreat from the hustle and bustle of everyday life, won't you relish the thought of spending time there with your beloved?"

✳ THE PERFECT CUP
OF TEA ✳

If you're a tea lover, when was the last time you were able to take the time to be really present while making a cup of tea? When making your next cup, relish the moment and pay attention to how much better your tea tastes after you slow down your mind and enjoy the process of this simple pleasure.

Fill the kettle with fresh cold water. Bring to a rolling boil. Scald the teapot with hot water, then empty. Place 1 rounded teaspoon of loose tea per cup into an infuser inside the pot (or one tea bag per cup). Pour boiling water into teapot. Let steep for three minutes. Remove tea infuser and serve.

✳ CANDY-COATED FUN ✳

I keep a great big candy bowl on my desk at work.
Most of my coworkers eventually end up there at some
point in the day, rummaging through the bowl for their
favorites. I always keep it filled with a variety of small,
individually wrapped items—gum, fireballs, peppermints,
lifesavers, chocolate, and lollipops—and make sure it's
all fresh. They enjoy the candy, and I enjoy the visits!

✳ BUTTERFLY KISSES ✳

Give someone you love butterfly kisses on the cheek
today. (And maybe you'll get some in return. Either
way is luscious.) In case you don't know how to do it,
it's easy—simply flutter your eyelashes across your
intended's cheek.

❃ INDULGE IN A
HEAD MASSAGE ❃

Giving a head massage is easy and requires no formal
training. All you need is someone who enjoys getting
their head rubbed and is willing to reciprocate. Stand
behind the person and place your hands very gently on
their head. Just rest there for a few seconds; the idea is
for the two of you to relax together and for you to get
in tune with them. If it is comfortable for them, have
them close their eyes. Place both hands on top of their
head, so your hands meet at the midline. Using all your
fingers, press and massage in circular motions, covering
the entire scalp from forehead to nape of neck and
from ear to ear. Ask them to guide you as to how much
pressure to apply. Use your thumbs on the spot where
the base of the skull meets the neck. Massage their
temples in a firm, circular motion for a minute. Slowly
massage your way across the forehead until your hands
meet in the middle. Return to the temples and bring
your hands down either side of their head to the point
in front of the earlobes where the jaw tends to clench.
Massage there. Finish off by gently pulling on their hair
in large sections and tugging upward.

❋ HIDE A LOVE NOTE ❋

My friend has had a troubled relationship with her father. But no matter how difficult things between them get, she always remembers that when she was in junior high and high school, after her mother had abandoned the family, her father often put an affectionate note in her backpack, which she would see as she took her books out at school. Those notes not only created joy in those moments, but they still do now, years later. Who in your life would be delighted to receive a surprise love note? Tuck one in a child's lunchbox, a loved one's bag, or under a pillow; it will bring both of you happiness.

❋ FLOWER GREETING CARDS ❋

Place pressed flowers that you've made or bought in a pattern you like on the front of blank cards or on stiff artists' paper available at craft or variety stores. Attach them to the paper with a dab of glue. Peel an appropriate amount of transparent, self-stick plastic film (like contact paper) from a roll and carefully place on top of the flowers, pressing from the center to the edge to eliminate air bubbles. Trim the edge of the plastic to match the card or paper. You can then send them to your friends for Christmas, Hanukkah, birthdays, Valentine's Day, or for no reason at all. Bookmarks can be made in exactly the same way—just cut the paper to an appropriate size.

❀ BLOOMING CARD ❀

Some creative person figured out how to plant seeds inside paper, and now a variety of places offer wonderful cards and notepaper that can be written on, mailed, and then planted either inside or out by your lucky letter recipient. Some of best ones I've seen are done by the Santa Fe Farmer's Market Cooperative Store; they're handmade from organic and recycled materials and studded with flowers, herbs, and vegetable seeds. The paper disintegrates when you plant it, and the seeds blossom into evidence of your feelings.

❋ SURPRISE SOMEONE ❋

My stepdaughter recently went to Europe. Just before she left, while she was in the bathroom, I snuck a hundred dollars into her backpack with a card saying it was "splurge" money. I had such fun thinking of the idea, finding the perfect hiding place, and trying not to get caught. It was so enjoyable that it didn't even matter to me if she appreciated the gesture or not! (She did! She found the treat days later while rooting around in her pack.) Put a little lift in your life and surprise someone you know.

❋ TOUCH-ME MASSAGE OIL ❋

- 4 OUNCES SWEET ALMOND OIL
- ½ TEASPOON OF YOUR FAVORITE ESSENTIAL OIL

Blend the oils well in a bowl and then pour into a small decorative glass bottle with a top. Add a beautiful ribbon, and you have a wonderful gift. Be sure to shake oils well before using.

✽ THE LOVE-NOTE JAR ✽

Here's a wonderful anniversary, holiday, birthday, or Valentine's Day idea. For the next special occasion, why not give your sweetheart a jar of love notes for their desk? Simply buy an attractive jar, put a beautiful ribbon around it, and fill it with notes from your heart—"I love you because you are so gentle and kind," "I am so grateful that you are in my life"—whatever is true for you. Your honey can open the jar to be reminded of your love whenever they are having a bad day or feeling unappreciated.

✽ MAKE A LOVE BOUQUET ✽

So many of us live far away from those we love. This is a simple pleasure adapted from *The Couple's Comfort Book* to bring those folks closer to you. Make a list of those who have been most important to you in your life. Then ask yourself, if they were a flower, what would they be? Then go to a florist and make a celebration bouquet out of all the flowers that represent your loved ones.

❋ DE-STRESSING TIME WITH KIDS ❋

The time you spend with your children may never resemble those cozy moments in TV commercials or others' online posts. But a few strategies may increase the pleasure. Are mornings a nightmare? Create a half hour in the evening to make lunches, collect books and other items for school, and choose clothes for the next day. Is homework a continual struggle? Help your children set up a study area. It will pay off to buy them "office" supplies, including dictionaries and other reference books. Plan to read, pay bills, and do your own office "homework" at the same time; that way, the children won't feel that you're enjoying TV while they're struggling with algebra.

To streamline dinnertime, one woman with teenage children assigned each of them one evening a week to plan the menu and prepare the meal. Whatever the results, at least it spares you from cooking. Is bedtime an agonizing series of delays? Settle on a time for children to be in bed, then let them read for as long as they like. They may stay awake later than you'd like at first, but at least they're in bed. And they should settle into getting the amount of sleep they need.

❋ "GET-IN-THE-MOOD" BATH ❋

Here's an aromatherapy bath to inspire sensuality and enhance sexual vitality. For added fun, take it with your love partner. Run a warm bath, and when the tub is nearly full, light some candles, turn off the lights, and add 15 drops cardamom oil, 10 drops ylang–ylang oil, and 10 drops patchouli oil. Relax into the water and surrender to the sensations.

❋ BE A JOHNNY TULIP BULB ❋

Plant a few bulbs in some public place: the median strip
outside your office, the corner of the park down the
street, the edge of the office parking lot. You'll have fun
now thinking of next spring when they suddenly burst
into color.

❋ FUN FIGHT ❋

This takes two people. Have a water, shaving cream, or
food fight in the kitchen. (It's the easiest place to clean
up.) If you're alone with your romantic partner, you
might want to try it in the nude. If you can't stand the
idea of a mess, consider a pillow fight instead. The point
is to let loose!

❋ THE KINDNESS BOX ❋

During the weeks leading up to the holidays, we keep a kindness box. We wrap up a shoebox like a present and cut a slot in the top. Then we put the box and a pencil and some paper under the tree. When someone in the family notices someone doing something kind, we write the act down on a piece of paper and put it in the box. (Young children could draw a picture or tell their parent what they saw and ask them to write it down.) On Christmas Eve, along with reading a beautiful picture book of the Christmas story, we open the box and read all the notes.

-

CHAPTER TEN

ESSENCE OF SELF-CARE

❋ FRAYED-NERVES BATH ❋

- 7 DROPS LAVENDER ESSENTIAL OIL
- 2 DROPS SWEET MARJORAM ESSENTIAL OIL
- 3 DROPS YLANG–YLANG ESSENTIAL OIL

Fill tub with warm water, and then add oils. Swish the oils around in the water to evenly disperse them, then submerge yourself.

❋ SLEEP POTION ❋

Here is a marvelous aromatherapy spray from Judith Fitzsimmons' and Paula M. Bousquet's wonderful book *Seasons of Aromatherapy*. Guaranteed to relax you and help you drift off.

- 2 DROPS CHAMOMILE ESSENTIAL OIL
- 4 DROPS LAVENDER ESSENTIAL OIL
- 3 DROPS ORANGE ESSENTIAL OIL
- 5 OUNCES WATER

Mix all ingredients together in a spray bottle. Spray bed linens, PJs or nightgown, and the air before bedtime.

❋ EYE PADS ❋

These are great for those of us who use our eyes a lot—and who doesn't? Lie down for a quarter of an hour with these covering your eyes, and presto—you'll feel rejuvenated in no time.

- 2 TEN–BY–TEN–INCH PIECES OF MUSLIN
- 4 OUNCES DRIED CHAMOMILE FLOWERS

With a pencil and ruler, mark off two-inch squares on both pieces of fabric, with ⅜-inch seam allowances around each square. You should have thirty-two squares. Place one of the pieces of muslin down and put 1 teaspoon chamomile in the center of each square. Cover with the other piece of fabric and pin. Sew along the guidelines you have made for yourself. Cut apart. Makes 16. To use, place 2 in a small bowl and pour 1 tablespoon of boiling water over pads. Cover and let sit until lukewarm. Squeeze gently and apply to closed eyelids for 15 minutes.

❋ LAVENDER BATH POWDER ❋

This is a delicious treat after a long soak in the tub.

- ⅓ CUP DRIED LAVENDER
- MORTAR AND PESTLE
- 1¼ CUPS CORNSTARCH
- 25 DROPS LAVENDER ESSENTIAL OIL
- SMALL BOX AND RIBBON

With a mortar and pestle, grind the lavender into a fine dust. Mix together with the cornstarch. Stirring constantly, slowly add the essential oil drops and mix well. Place in a beautiful box and tie with a ribbon.

❋ THE DELIGHTS OF SCENT ❋

From time immemorial, scent has been used as an aphrodisiac. Time–tested fragrances include amber, ambergris, jasmine, lily of the valley, musk, myrrh, orange blossom, patchouli, sandalwood, and tuberose. You might also try using essential oils in a diffuser in the bedroom or burning incense.

❋ HAIR MOISTURIZER ❋

Rosemary is very good for hair, particularly dark hair, to which it imparts a wonderful shine. It will also help cut down on the problem of flyaway hair. This recipe makes enough for several applications.

- 8 DROPS CEDAR ESSENTIAL OIL
- 8 DROPS LAVENDER ESSENTIAL OIL
- 12 DROPS ROSEMARY ESSENTIAL OIL
- 2 TABLESPOONS OLIVE OIL

In a small glass container, mix the essential oils together. Add the olive oil. Pour about a teaspoon into the palm of your hand and rub hands together. Massage your head, hair, and scalp with the blend. Put a shower cap or warm towel on your head over the nourishing oils and leave it on for fifteen minutes. Wash and rinse your hair twice.

❋ PINE BATH OIL ❋

This oil is a great skin softener. Just pour a bit into your bath under the running water.

- 1 CLUSTER PINE NEEDLES
- 1 CUP BABY OIL, APPROXIMATELY

Put the pine needles in a glass container with a lid. Cover completely with baby oil and cover tightly. Store in a dry, cool place for 4 weeks. Strain the oil, and decant into an attractive glass bottle. If you'd like, you can add fresh pine needles for decoration. Makes 1 cup.

❊ CALMING BATH ❊

The sensual delight of taking a bath in aromatic oils goes back to the Romans, who raised bathing to a high art. The public baths consisted of three parts: first you went to the unctuarium, where you were anointed in oils. Then you proceeded to the frigidarium, where you took a cold bath, then to the tepidarium for a tepid one. You finished with a hot bath in the caldarium. While we don't bathe as the Romans did, we can indulge in the essence of the practice.

- 4 DROPS BERGAMOT ESSENTIAL OIL
- 4 DROPS LAVENDER ESSENTIAL OIL
- 2 DROPS CLARY SAGE ESSENTIAL OIL

Run a warm bath. Drop the essential oils into the stream of water. Slide in and relax for 10 to 15 minutes.

❊ HERBAL SOAP BALLS ❊

Here's an easy, inexpensive homemade gift that
the little ones can help with. The kids will love the
pulverizing, and recipients will like its clean fragrance.

- 1 TABLESPOON DRIED HERBS, PULVERIZED
  (YOU CAN USE ROSEMARY, SAGE, THYME,
  PEPPERMINT, OR A COMBINATION)
- 5 DROPS MATCHING ESSENTIAL OIL
- 1 PERSONAL-SIZE IVORY SOAP BAR, SHREDDED
  AND PLACED IN A MIXING BOWL

Prepare your dried herbs by pulverizing them if they are
not already in that form; you can either use a mortar and
pestle or, if you do not have one, crush the herbs down
on a clean cutting board or plate beneath the back of a
spoon until they are powdered or nearly so. Pour ¼ cup
boiling water over the herbs and add the essential oil.
Let steep for 20 minutes. Bring this mixture to a boil
and pour over the soap. When cool enough, mix well by
hand and let stand for 15 minutes. Mix again and form
into 3 balls. Place on plastic wrap and let stand for 3
days. Makes 3 soap balls.

❀ SENSUAL BATH ❀

This bath feels luxurious beyond belief.

- 2 DROPS CEDAR ESSENTIAL OIL
- 2 DROPS CLARY SAGE ESSENTIAL OIL
- 2 DROPS LAVENDER ESSENTIAL OIL
- 2 DROPS ORANGE ESSENTIAL OIL
- 2 TABLESPOONS VEGETABLE OIL

Combine all oils and pour the mixture into the stream of
a warm bath.

❀ STEAMING TEA FACIAL ❀

- 1 CHAMOMILE TEA BAG
- 1 PEPPERMINT TEA BAG
- 3 CUPS BOILING WATER

Place the tea bags in a large, wide-mouthed bowl or
pot. Add boiling water and allow to cool for 2 minutes.
Place a clean towel over your head and the bowl,
keeping your face at least eight inches away from the
surface of the hot water, and steam for 10 minutes.

❋ CITRUS TONER ❋

This toner is great for oily or normal skin.

- ¼ CUP LEMON PEEL, FINELY GRATED
- ¼ CUP GRAPEFRUIT PEEL, FINELY GRATED
- 1 CUP MINT LEAVES
- 1 CUP WATER

Heat water in a small saucepan on high heat. Add mint and citrus peelings to rapidly boiling water. Continue to boil for 1 to 2 minutes, or until peels become soft and slightly translucent. Remove from heat. Cool and strain. Store in the refrigerator or freezer; it will last 2 to 3 weeks.

❀ FLORAL SPLASH ❀

With so many real essential oils available these days, it's easy to make your own eau de cologne. Here's one version, but feel free to experiment with the essential oils of your choice. If you find this concoction too strong, just dilute it with bottled water. A beautiful antique bottle makes the perfect receptacle.

- ½ CUP 100–PROOF VODKA
- STERILIZED WIDE–NECK GLASS JAR WITH TOP
- 20 DROPS ORANGE ESSENTIAL OIL
- 10 DROPS BERGAMOT ESSENTIAL OIL
- 10 DROPS LEMON ESSENTIAL OIL
- 2 DROPS NEROLI ESSENTIAL OIL
- ¼ CUP UNFLAVORED BOTTLED WATER (STILL WATER—THAT IS, WITHOUT CARBONATION)
- PAPER COFFEE FILTER
- STERILIZED DECORATIVE GLASS BOTTLE WITH TOP THAT CAN HOLD ¾ CUP

Pour the vodka into the wide–mouthed jar, then add the essential oils and stir with a new wooden spoon. Put lid on and let stand for 2 days. Add the water and stir. Cover again and let sit for 4 to 6 weeks. Strain through coffee filter and pour into decorative bottle.

❋ MINTY FACIAL
ASTRINGENT ❋

- 1 TABLESPOON FRESH PEPPERMINT OR
  SPEARMINT LEAVES
- 1 CUP WITCH HAZEL

Combine ingredients in a jar with a tight-fitting lid.
Steep in a cool, dry place for one week, shaking
occasionally. Strain and pour liquid into a bottle or
spritzer. Use about 1 teaspoon a day on your face.
Good for normal and oily skin. Makes about a six-
week supply.

❋ STEAMING CLEAN ❋

You don't need to go to a spa or to buy any fancy
equipment to enjoy a facial steam. All you need is a
large pot of boiling water, a sturdy table, a handful of
herbs, and a bath towel. Bring a large pot of water to a
boil. Remove from heat and add a handful each of whole
sage leaves, whole peppermint leaves, and chamomile
flowers. Carry the pot over to the table along with the
bath towel and sit down in front of the pot. Drape the

towel over your head and shoulders so that you and the pot are under the towel, being sure to keep your face at least a foot away from the pot. Breathe slowly and deeply through the nose, lifting the towel to get fresh air as needed. Stay under the towel tent for 5 to 10 minutes. When you're done, moisturize your face with a good lotion. This practice is not recommended if you have extremely dry skin, heart trouble, or breathing problems such as asthma; although some swear by it for breathing difficulties, check first with your physician to be safe.

❋ HERBAL SKIN CLEANERS ❋

Many dried herbs are good for the skin. Here are the best herbs for various purposes and skin types:

- *RELAXING:* CHAMOMILE, LAVENDER, ST. JOHN'S WORT
- *SOFTENING:* CHAMOMILE, LAVENDER, ROSE, ST. JOHN'S WORT
- *CLEANSING:* ARNICA, CALENDULA, CHAMOMILE, COMFREY, ELDERFLOWER, LAVENDER, NETTLE, PEPPERMINT, ROSEMARY, YARROW

- *SOOTHING:* ARNICA, CALENDULA, CHAMOMILE, ELDERFLOWER, GREEN TEA, LAVENDER, ROSE, WITCH HAZEL
- *STIMULATING:* GINGKO BILOBA, NETTLE, PEPPERMINT, ROSEMARY
- *NOURISHING:* COMFREY, GINKGO BILOBA, GINSENG, ST. JOHN'S WORT
- *REJUVENATING:* ARNICA, CALENDULA, CHAMOMILE, COMFREY, GREEN TEA, GINKGO BILOBA, GINSENG, LAVENDER, ROSEMARY

Decide what kind of herbal mixture you need for your face. Then soak 1 heaping teaspoon of an herb or blend of herbs in a cup of whole, unpasteurized milk. Store the mixture in the refrigerator for a few hours, then strain, saving the milk. To use, rinse your face in warm water, then use cotton balls to apply the milk to face, avoiding eyes. Rinse first with warm water and then with cool.

❄ ELDERFLOWER SKIN REFRESHER ❄

If you live in an area where elderflowers grow, here's a recipe for an old-fashioned skin tonic. This makes a great gift when packaged in a beautiful glass bottle decorated with an old botanical illustration of an elderflower, which may be as easy to find as a quick internet search and a little printing time. Be sure to include storage instructions if you give it as a gift.

- 50 ELDERFLOWER HEADS, WASHED IN COLD WATER
- 1 QUART JAR, STERILIZED
- 2½ CUPS WATER
- 5 TABLESPOONS VODKA
- CHEESECLOTH
- DECORATIVE GLASS BOTTLES WITH CAPS

Remove petals from heads, making sure not to bruise the flowers; do not include stems. Place petals in quart jar. Boil water and slowly pour over flowers. Let stand for 30 minutes and add vodka. Cover and let stand on counter for 24 hours. Pour liquid through cheesecloth into glass bottles and cap. Store in a cool, dry, dark place like a cabinet until opened and used.

Then keep in the refrigerator and use within one month.
Makes 3 cups.

❊ MINT FOOT SCRUB ❊

- 1 CUP UNFLAVORED YOGURT
- 1 CUP KOSHER OR ROCK SALT
- ¾ CUP MINT LEAVES

Combine ingredients and apply the mixture to your feet.
Use a damp washcloth to gently scrub rough spots.
Rinse feet and then apply a thick lotion.

❋ SALT GLOW ❋

This lotion is fabulous for exfoliating dead skin, particularly when your tan is starting to flake. Be sure not to use on your face or neck; it's too rough for that.

- 2 CUPS SEA SALT
- 7 DROPS OF YOUR FAVORITE ESSENTIAL OIL
- 1 OUNCE SWEET ALMOND OIL

Place salt and oils in a bowl and combine well with your fingers. Stand or sit naked in an empty bathtub and rub salt mixture into your skin with your hands, starting with your feet. Massage in a circular motion. As the salts fall, pick up and reuse until you reach your neck, making sure not to scrub areas with the most sensitive skin. Then fill the tub with warm water and soak.

❊ SUMMER FACIAL TONER ❊

Here's an easy, all-natural skin freshener, a perfect pick-me-up for hot, humid weather.

- 1½ CUPS WITCH HAZEL EXTRACT
- ½ CUP ROSE WATER
- 1 TABLESPOON GRATED LIME PEEL
- 1 TABLESPOON DRIED ROSEMARY LEAVES
- 2 DROPS LAVENDER OIL
- 2 DROPS ROSEMARY OIL

Combine the witch hazel and rose water in a clean glass jar with a tight-fitting lid. Shake well. Add the remaining ingredients and again shake well, this time for five minutes. Store the jar in a dark, cool place, shaking five minutes a day for two weeks. At the end of that period, strain the mixture and store the remaining liquid in an airtight container, where it will last up to six weeks if refrigerated. For extra refreshment, try keeping a spritz bottle full of toner chilled, and use it straight from the refrigerator.

❋ HEADACHE PILLOW ❋

This is a Midwestern pioneer recipe

- ½ OUNCE GROUND CLOVES
- 2 OUNCES DRIED LAVENDER
- 2 OUNCES DRIED MARJORAM
- 2 OUNCES DRIED ROSE PETALS
- 1 TEASPOON ORRIS ROOT
- 2 PIECES OF COTTON BATTING, EACH SLIGHTLY SMALLER THAN A HANDKERCHIEF
- 2 HANDKERCHIEFS
- OPTIONAL: LACE OR RIBBON

Grind spices, flowers, and orris root together, either with a mortar and pestle or in a food processor. Pack the powder in between the two pieces of cotton batting. Sew together three sides of the two handkerchiefs. Place the cotton "pillow" inside and hand sew the fourth side tight enough that the contents don't leak out. Decorate with lace or ribbons if desired. To use, lie on pillow, perhaps tucked under your cheek, and inhale fragrance or place it over your eyes.

✳ HOMEMADE MINT LIP BALM ✳

The microwave makes this a snap.

- 1 POUND JAR PETROLEUM JELLY
- 1 MICROWAVE–SAFE QUART CONTAINER
- 2 TABLESPOONS DRIED MINT, FINELY PULVERIZED
- 1 OUNCE SHREDDED BEESWAX (AVAILABLE AT CRAFT STORES)
- PIECE OF CHEESECLOTH
- 1 QUART CONTAINER WITH SPOUT
- 1 OUNCE ALOE VERA
- 20 DROPS LIQUID VITAMIN E
- 2 TABLESPOONS WITCH HAZEL
- TINY REUSABLE CONTAINERS WITH LIDS (AVAILABLE AT HARDWARE OR CRAFT STORES)

Take the petroleum jelly out of its jar and place in a microwave–safe quart container. Set the microwave on 50 percent power and heat until the petroleum jelly is soft. Put the mint and the beeswax into the jelly and heat for one minute. Stir the jelly, then heat again for another minute. (Note: Stir with a nonmetal spoon so as to not flavor the liquid.) Repeat until completely melted. Take the cheesecloth and fold it in half. Strain the beeswax and petroleum jelly mixture through the cheesecloth into the quart container with spout. Discard cheesecloth. Stir in the remaining ingredients and pour into containers. Fills several containers, depending on size.

❋ MOOD-ENHANCING SPRAY ❋

If the dark days of late fall are dragging you down, consider this little pick–me–up—an easy–to–make rose room spray. Besides being the classic scent of romance, rose is said to have antidepressant properties; lavender and bergamot are also mood lifters.

Simply combine 4 drops of rose essential oil, 2 drops of bergamot essential oil, 2 drops of lavender, and 1 cup of water. Place in small plastic spray bottle, shake well, and spray the room.

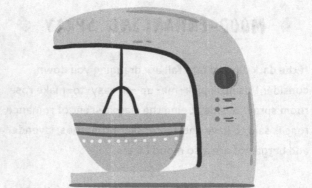

-

CHAPTER ELEVEN

RECIPES TO SAVOR

❋ CRANBERRY VINEGAR ❋

You've heard of raspberry vinegar, but what about
cranberry? It's great on salads and chicken dishes.
Wash and pick over the cranberries, then thoroughly pat
dry using clean towels. Use 1 cup of fresh cranberries
per quart of vinegar. Pack the cranberries into clean
bottles or jars with lids or corks, and fill each container
with white wine vinegar that has been heated just to
the boiling point. Cork or cap them after filling, then set
them on a sunny windowsill for about two weeks (four
weeks if it's not very sunny). The warmth of the sun will
infuse the vinegar with the cranberry flavor. Do a taste
test; if the vinegar doesn't seem flavorful enough, strain
it and add more cranberries. When it suits you, label
and decorate the jars with a beautiful ribbon. Store at
room temperature.

✳ PERFECT
MASHED POTATOES ✳

Potatoes are high on the list of universal comfort foods.
And what could be more basic than good old mashed
potatoes? This recipe comes from Jane and Michael
Stern's *Square Meals: A Cookbook*. The authors claim
to have found the best way to make perfect mashed
potatoes. See what you think.

- 2 POUNDS MEDIUM POTATOES, PEELED
  AND HALVED
- ½ CUP MILK
- ¼ CUP HEAVY CREAM
- 3 TABLESPOONS BUTTER
- SALT AND PEPPER TO TASTE

Boil potatoes in rapidly boiling salted water until you
can pierce them easily with a fork. Drain and return
potatoes to pot, then reheat until all moisture is
evaporated, being careful not to let them burn. Transfer
to mixing bowl and mash well. Combine milk and cream
in a small bowl and pour into potatoes while continuing
to mash. Add butter, salt, and pepper to taste. Serve
immediately. Serves 4 to 6.

✳ CHOCOLATE PUDDING ✳

There is nothing like chocolate pudding made from
scratch! It's quite simple to make. If you are a fan of
the "skin" of the pudding, chill uncovered (the longer
you chill it, the thicker it will get). If you dislike the skin,
cover the pudding tightly and serve as soon as it's cold.

- 4 TABLESPOONS COCOA
- 4 TABLESPOONS CORNSTARCH
- ⅔ CUP SUGAR
- ¼ TEASPOON SALT
- 2 CUPS LIGHT CREAM
- 1 TEASPOON VANILLA EXTRACT

In the top of a double boiler over hot but not boiling
water, combine cocoa, cornstarch, sugar, and salt. Add
½ cup cream and stir until smooth. Stir remaining cream
in slowly, stirring constantly, until thick. Stir in vanilla.
Pour into container and chill. Serves 4.

❋ HANDMADE PRETZELS ❋

Pretzels are great snacks that can easily be made at home. The longer you knead the dough, the softer the pretzel will be. If you've got kids, enlist them—to make the process more fun, the dough can easily be formed in the shapes of letters and numbers.

- 1½ CUPS WARM WATER
- 4 CUPS FLOUR
- 1 PACKAGE YEAST
- 1 TEASPOON SALT, PLUS MORE FOR ON TOP OF PRETZELS
- 1 TABLESPOON SUGAR
- 1 EGG, BEATEN

Preheat oven to 425°F. Put the warm water into a large bowl, sprinkle in yeast, and stir until it dissolves. Add sugar, flour, and salt. Mix well, then knead dough until it is smooth and soft. Roll and twist dough into desired shapes—letters, numbers, twists, and so on. Grease two cookie sheets. Lay the pretzel dough shapes onto cookie sheets. Brush with beaten egg and sprinkle lightly with salt. Bake for 12 to 15 minutes, or until golden. Makes 1 to 2 dozen, depending on size.

❋ CRAVING CRACKERS ❋

Crackers are incredibly easy to make, and homemade ones are so much better than store-bought ones. I love sesame seeds, so I sprinkle some on just before baking—you can too!

- 2 CUPS ALL-PURPOSE FLOUR
- 1 TEASPOON BAKING POWDER
- SALT
- ¾ CUP WATER, APPROXIMATELY
- 4 TABLESPOONS BUTTER, MARGARINE, OR OTHER SHORTENING
- OPTIONAL: SESAME SEEDS

Preheat oven to 325°F. Sift together flour, baking powder, and a pinch of salt. With two knives, cut the shortening into the flour until mixture is fine. Add just enough water to make a firm dough. On a lightly floured surface, roll out thinly with a floured rolling pin. Using a round cookie cutter, stamp out crackers, prick them all over with a fork, and sprinkle with salt and sesame seeds if desired. Bake on a lightly greased cookie sheet for 20 minutes or until crisp. Cool on a rack and store in airtight container. Makes 2 dozen.

✲ GARLIC SPREAD ✲

Years ago, independent filmmaker Les Blank made a movie called *Garlic Is as Good as Ten Mothers*. If you agree, you should try this confit. Slather it on sourdough baguettes or use it any time a recipe calls for cooked garlic. And don't forget to use the leftover garlic-infused oil. If you have a large garlic crop or make a trip to the farmers' market and come upon an abundance of it at a bargain price, you can package this up in gift jars for friends as well as for yourself.

- 8 OUNCES FRESH GARLIC CLOVES, PEELED
- 2 CUPS OLIVE OIL
- STERILIZED JARS WITH LIDS THAT SEAL

In a medium saucepan, bring the garlic and oil to a simmer and cook over low heat for 25 to 30 minutes or until garlic is very tender. Cool and pack into containers. Store in refrigerator and use within two weeks. Makes 2 pounds.

❋ MEXICAN HOT CHOCOLATE ❋

This drink is divine, the perfect thing for a cold evening.
If you can find cinnamon-flavored Ibarra chocolate,
use it instead of the semisweet chocolate and omit the
cinnamon and brown sugar.

- 4 CUPS MILK
- 3 THREE-INCH LONG CINNAMON STICKS,
  BROKEN IN HALF
- 30 WHOLE CLOVES
- 1 TEASPOON ANISEED
- 5 OUNCES SEMISWEET CHOCOLATE, CHOPPED
- 2 TABLESPOONS UNSWEETENED
  COCOA POWDER
- 2 TABLESPOONS BROWN SUGAR

In a large, heavy saucepan over medium heat, bring the
milk, cinnamon, cloves, and aniseed to a simmer. Add
the remaining ingredients and whisk until the chocolate
melts. Remove from heat, cover, and let steep for 45
minutes. Gently warm before serving; using a double
boiler is the most foolproof method. Serves 4.

❋ HOMEMADE
FLOUR TORTILLAS ❋

My husband swears by these.

- 4 CUPS FLOUR
- 1¼ TEASPOON SALT
- 6 TABLESPOONS VEGETABLE SHORTENING
- APPROXIMATELY 1¼ CUPS BOILING WATER

Sift together the flour and salt into a large bowl. Mix
the shortening in by hand until the mixture resembles
cornmeal and feels slightly gritty to the touch. Stir in
enough boiling water that the dough sticks together.
Place the dough on a floured surface and knead for
approximately 5 minutes. Form dough into a ball, place
inside the bowl, and cover with plastic wrap. After
approximately 30 minutes, divide the dough into 10
to 12 balls, then roll each ball flat with a well-floured
rolling pin. Cook in a cast-iron skillet over medium
heat, about 20 seconds on each side. Makes 10 to
12 tortillas.

✳ OLD-FASHIONED RICE PUDDING ✳

Here's a warming treat, one that's especially good for the March doldrums. And it couldn't be easier to make.

- 3½ CUPS MILK
- ½ CUP SUGAR, DIVIDED INTO TWO ¼ CUP PORTIONS
- ½ TEASPOON CINNAMON
- ½ CUP LONG GRAIN RICE
- 2 EGG YOLKS
- ½ CUP WHIPPING CREAM
- 1 TEASPOON VANILLA

Heat milk, ¼ cup sugar, and cinnamon in saucepan just to a boil; stir in rice and reduce heat to low. Cover and simmer for 35 to 45 minutes. In a separate bowl, whisk egg yolks, cream, ¼ cup sugar, and vanilla. Add gradually to rice. Bring to a boil and cook, stirring, for 3 minutes longer. Makes 4 servings.

❋ MEXICAN WEDDING COOKIES ❋

Traditional wedding cookies are often served at other festive occasions as well.

- ½ CUP POWDERED SUGAR
- 1 CUP BUTTER, SOFTENED
- 1 TEASPOON VANILLA
- 2¼ CUPS FLOUR
- ¼ TEASPOON SALT
- ADDITIONAL POWDERED SUGAR
- OPTIONAL: ¾ CUP CHOPPED NUTS

Cream together the sugar, butter, and vanilla in a large bowl. Sift in the flour and salt and stir to combine. Add the nuts, if using. Cover and chill the dough for 2 hours in the refrigerator or 10 minutes in the freezer. Preheat oven to 400°F. Roll the dough into one-inch balls and place on an ungreased cookie sheet. Bake until set, about 10 minutes. While still warm, roll the cookies in powdered sugar. Makes 2 dozen.

✳ TEN-MINUTE FUDGE ✳

Ah, chocolate!

- 9 SQUARES (1 OUNCE EACH)
  UNSWEETENED CHOCOLATE
- 4 TABLESPOONS BUTTER
- 4½ CUPS SIFTED POWDERED SUGAR
- ⅓ CUP INSTANT NONFAT DRY MILK
- ½ CUP LIGHT OR DARK CORN SYRUP
- 1 TABLESPOON WATER
- 1 TEASPOON VANILLA
- OPTIONAL: ½ CUP CHOPPED NUTS

Grease an eight-inch square pan. Melt chocolate and butter in the top of a 2-quart double boiler over hot water. Meanwhile, sift together sugar and dry milk in a medium bowl. Stir corn syrup, water, and vanilla extract into chocolate-butter mixture. Stir in sifted sugar and dry milk in two additions. Continue stirring until mixture is well blended and smooth. Remove from heat. Stir in nuts if desired. Pour mixture into pan. Let cool, then cut into squares. Makes 24 two-inch squares.

❄ CARAMEL APPLES ❄

These make a wonderful summer party treat—one that all your friends must make for themselves! Be careful to let them cool completely before eating as caramel has a tendency to cool slowly.

- 4 MEDIUM APPLES
- SMALL BOWL MELTED BUTTER
- SMALL BOWL BROWN SUGAR
- OPTIONAL: FINELY CHOPPED PEANUTS

Place each apple on a shish-kebab skewer. Hold it over the coals, turning frequently, until the skin can be pulled off. Without removing it from the skewer, peel each apple, then dip it in butter, and then in brown sugar, covering completely. Hold skewer over grill and slowly turn until sugar becomes caramelized. Dip in peanuts if desired, and cool completely. Serves 4.

✳ HOMEMADE VANILLA
ICE CREAM ✳

When the French novelist Stendhal first tasted ice cream, he declared, "What a pity this isn't a sin!" Judge for yourself.

- 3 CUPS HALF-AND-HALF
- ¾ CUP SUGAR
- 6 EGG YOLKS
- 2 TEASPOONS VANILLA EXTRACT

In a heavy saucepan, bring the half-and-half to a simmer over medium heat, being careful not to boil it. In a heatproof bowl, whisk together the sugar and egg yolks until well blended. Gradually pour the hot half-and-half into the egg mixture, whisking continuously. Return mixture to saucepan and cook over medium-low heat, stirring with a wooden spoon, until the custard is thick enough to coat a spoon, about 5 minutes.

Pour the custard through a strainer into a clean bowl and refrigerate until cold. Transfer the custard to an ice cream freezer or ice cream maker and follow manufacturer's instructions for freezing. If possible,

let stand 2 or 3 hours at freezing temperature before
serving. Makes about 5 cups.

❋ ROCK CANDY ❋

Remember this old-fashioned candy? Making it is a
great kid-friendly cooking project.

- 1 CUP SUGAR
- 1 CUP WATER
- 1 TEASPOON VANILLA, PEPPERMINT, OR OTHER
  FLAVORING OF YOUR CHOICE (OPTIONAL)
- WOODEN SKEWERS ABOUT THREE
  INCHES LONG
- SMALL WIDE-NECKED GLASS BOTTLES OR JARS
  (LIKE THE KIND APPLE JUICE OFTEN COMES IN)
- FOOD COLORING
- ALUMINUM FOIL

Boil water and sugar, stirring occasionally until sugar
is completely dissolved. Add flavoring if desired. Pour
into bottles or jars, then add food coloring, one color
per jar, stirring with a wooden skewer. Cover the jar top
with foil, then poke a wooden skewer through the foil

into each jar. Let sit until sugar water has cooled and crystals have formed. Voilà—rock candy. Makes 1 cup; quantity varies depending on number of jars.

❋ GENUINE CHOCOLATE MALT ❋

If you prefer vanilla, omit the chocolate syrup. Either way, be sure your malted milk powder is not chocolate flavored.

- 4 SCOOPS VANILLA ICE CREAM
- 1½ CUPS MILK
- 3 TABLESPOONS CHOCOLATE SYRUP
- 1 TEASPOON VANILLA EXTRACT
- 2 TABLESPOONS MALTED MILK POWDER

Whip up all ingredients in blender. Serves 1.

❋ SUREFIRE RHUBARB-STRAWBERRY CRISP ❋

Summer is the time for this treat.

- 3 CUPS RHUBARB, SLICED
- 2 CUPS STRAWBERRIES, WHOLE OR SLICED
- JUICE OF ONE LEMON
- 1 STICK BUTTER, SOFTENED
- 1 CUP GRANULATED SUGAR
- 1 CUP FLOUR

Preheat oven to 400°F. Combine rhubarb, strawberries, and lemon juice in a nine-by-thirteen-inch baking pan. In a medium bowl, combine the butter, sugar, and flour until crumbly, then spread the crumble mixture over the fruit. Bake uncovered for 20 minutes or until crisp is bubbly and top is browned. Serves 6.

❋ HOMEMADE GINGER ALE ❋

This ale is very simple to make, but you've got to drink it up after you make it—the carbonation won't last long, and it shouldn't be sealed or it could explode.

- 3 TABLESPOONS GINGER ROOT, PEELED
- 4 QUARTS BOILING WATER
- 1 LIME
- 3 CUPS SUGAR
- 3 TABLESPOONS CREAM OF TARTAR
- 1 TABLESPOON YEAST

Pound the ginger until it is a mash. Pour the boiling water over it, and add the lime, sugar, and cream of tartar. Cover with a cloth and let cool until it is lukewarm. Add yeast; let rest 6 hours. Chill, strain, and serve. Makes 4 quarts.

❋ PLENTY OF PESTO ❋

No book on simple pleasures would be complete without a pesto recipe. Pesto is usually made with basil, but it can also be made with cilantro or parsley or a combination. All you need is a large quantity of fresh herbs. Pesto can be frozen and lasts for several months in the freezer. If your basil is going to seed, make a large batch of pesto minus the cheese and freeze it. When you use it later, simply add the Parmesan.

- ¾ CUP OLIVE OIL
- 1 CLOVE GARLIC
- 1 TABLESPOON PINE NUTS
- ¼ TEASPOON SALT
- ⅓ CUP GRATED PARMESAN CHEESE
- 4 CUPS BASIL, CILANTRO, OR
  PARSLEY, WASHED

Place all the ingredients except the basil in a food processor. Process until smooth. Add the basil a little at a time until pesto is smooth. Makes 1 cup or a little more.

❊ ROSE WINE ❊

Here's an old-fashioned treat. (Don't use this recipe if you spray your roses with insecticide.) Be sure to thoroughly clean the roses, and do not store your wine in metal containers or stir with metal utensils; metal reacts to the acid in wine.

- 2 ORANGES
- 3 QUARTS ROSE PETALS, WASHED AND
  LIGHTLY PACKED

- 1 GALLON BOILING WATER
- 3 POUNDS SUGAR
- 1 PACKAGE YEAST
- 5 WHITE PEPPERCORNS

Peel the rind from the oranges and set the oranges aside; cut up rind. Place the rose petals in a large saucepan. Pour the boiling water in and add the orange rind and sugar. Boil for 20 minutes; remove from heat and cool. Add the yeast dissolved in warm water per package instructions, the juice from the oranges, and the peppercorns. Pour into a stoneware crock, cover, and let sit where temperature is between 60 and 80°F for two weeks. Strain, discarding petals, rinds, and peppercorns, and bottle in sterilized jars, corking lightly, for about 3 months or until the wine has completed fermenting. To store wine, seal bottles with paraffin. Makes about 1 gallon.

❋ CHINESE ALMOND COOKIES ❋

These are simply delicious.

- ½ CUP WHOLE ROASTED ALMONDS
- 1 CUP SIFTED ALL-PURPOSE FLOUR
- ½ TEASPOON BAKING POWDER
- ¼ TEASPOON SALT
- ½ CUP BUTTER OR MARGARINE
- ⅓ CUP GRANULATED SUGAR
- ½ TEASPOON ALMOND EXTRACT
- 1 TABLESPOON GIN, VODKA, OR WATER

Preheat oven to 350°F and grease several cookie
sheets. Reserve 36 whole almonds; finely chop or grind
remainder. Sift flour with baking powder and salt.
Thoroughly cream butter and sugar in a large bowl.
Stir in all remaining ingredients except whole almonds.
Form dough into 24 balls and place on greased cookie
sheets, making sure they have space between them.
Press a whole almond in the center of each ball, or dot
with a bit of red food coloring. Bake for 20 minutes or
until lightly browned. Makes about 2 dozen.

❋ CONE CAKES ❋

This is a fun way to serve cake. You can be sure that the kids will be clamoring for more than one.

- 24 FLAT-BOTTOMED ICE CREAM CONES
- 1 PACKAGE (17 TO 24 OUNCES) CAKE MIX
- MUFFIN TINS
- FROSTING AND CAKE DECORATIONS OF YOUR CHOICE

Prepare the cake batter according to cake mix package directions. Spoon the batter into the cones until they are two-thirds full. Place the cones in the muffin tins and bake according to package directions for cupcakes. When cones are cool, frost and decorate. Makes 24.

❋ APLETS ❋

Here's a recipe for a classic candy that is quite easy to make on your own.

- 2 CUPS APPLESAUCE
- 2 CUPS SUGAR

- 2 TABLESPOONS UNFLAVORED GELATIN
- ½ CUP COLD WATER
- 1½ CUPS CHOPPED ALMONDS, WALNUTS, OR OTHER NUTS IF YOU LIKE
- 3 DROPS ORANGE EXTRACT
- POWDERED SUGAR

Butter an eight-inch baking pan. Cook applesauce and sugar in a medium saucepan over medium heat, stirring often, until it gets very thick. While applesauce is cooking, sprinkle the gelatin into the ½ cup of water and let stand. Remove applesauce from heat, and stir in gelatin. Add almonds and orange extract and stir well. Pour into baking pan. Cover and let stand on the counter overnight; do not refrigerate. The next day, cut into squares and roll in powdered sugar. Will keep up to a week or so. Serves 12.

❋ PEANUT BRITTLE ❋

If you like peanut brittle, you must make your own!

- ¼ CUP WATER
- 1 CUP SUGAR

- ¼ TEASPOON CREAM OF TARTAR
- ½ CUP LIGHT CORN SYRUP
- 1½ CUPS ROASTED, UNSALTED PEANUTS
- 1 TABLESPOON PEANUT BUTTER
- ½ TEASPOON SALT
- ½ TEASPOON BAKING SODA

Grease a large cookie sheet. In a large saucepan, bring the water to a boil and add the sugar and cream of tartar. Stir until sugar is dissolved. Stir in the corn syrup, place a candy thermometer in the pan, and cook over medium-high heat until temperature reaches 350°F. Remove from heat and stir in remaining ingredients. Pour onto prepared sheet; you can line the baking sheet with waxed paper beforehand to make lifting the brittle off it easier. Let cool completely, then break into pieces. Store in an airtight container for up to 1 week. Makes about 1 pound.

❋ HOMEMADE ORANGE OR LEMON PEEL ❋

This is a nineteenth-century confection that makes a great housewarming gift.

- 2 QUARTS PLUS 1 CUP BOTTLED WATER (NOT TAP WATER; USE FILTERED OR SPRING WATER)
- 2 TABLESPOONS KOSHER SALT
- RIND FROM 10 NAVEL ORANGES OR 15 LEMONS, HALVED OR QUARTERED
- 4 CUPS GRANULATED SUGAR
- SUPERFINE SUGAR

Combine 1 quart of water with the salt in a medium saucepan and bring to a boil. Boil for 5 minutes covered and set aside. When cool, pour into a large jar, add the rinds and store covered in refrigerator for 6 days. Pour the brine into a saucepan with room to spare and bring to a boil. Reduce heat, add rinds, and poach on medium low heat for 10 minutes. Drain rinds thoroughly using a strainer and discard liquid. Combine 1 quart of water and 2 cups sugar. Bring to a boil, add rinds, and boil for 30 minutes or until peels start to look clear around the edges. Drain rinds in colander. Cut rinds into strips. Combine remaining 1 cup water and 2 cups sugar. Bring to a boil and add rinds. Boil gently until syrup candies on the strips. Remove the strips with a slotted spoon and spread them to dry on racks. Drying time will vary depending on weather but usually takes a day. When strips are dry, dust lightly with superfine sugar and store in airtight containers. Makes 1 pound.

CHAPTER TWELVE

-

SEASONAL COMFORTS

❋ MAPLE CANDY ❋

Heavy snowfalls are blessings for people who love maple candy. The good news is that you don't need an acre of sugar maples and a bucket of sap to make it: a bottle of maple syrup will do just fine.

- ½ CUP MAPLE SYRUP
- 1 BAKING PAN FULL OF PACKED, CLEAN SNOW

Leave the packed pan of clean snow either outside or in the freezer until you're ready to use it. Then heat the maple syrup in a pot to 270°F (check with a candy thermometer). Carefully dribble the hot syrup in small patches over the snow. Each one of these patches will magically turn to maple candy. Yum!

❋ SNOW ICE CREAM ❋

This is a wonderful nineteenth-century treat that you can replicate if you live in snowy climes.

- 1 CUP HEAVY CREAM
- ¼ CUP SUPERFINE SUGAR

- 2 TEASPOONS LEMON EXTRACT OR TWO TABLESPOONS ROSEWATER
- 8 TO 10 CUPS FRESH, CLEAN SNOW

Mix the cream, sugar, and lemon extract or rosewater. Add the snow a little at a time, beating with a whisk, using only enough snow to make a stiff ice cream. Serve immediately. Makes 8 servings.

❋ CRANBERRY TEA ❋

This is a wonderfully spicy potion. The recipe makes enough for a crowd. You can make it with decaf tea bags if you want to avoid the caffeine kick.

- 4 CUPS WATER
- 4 CUPS CRANBERRY JUICE
- 4 ORANGE PEKOE TEA BAGS
- ¾ TEASPOON CINNAMON
- 16 WHOLE CLOVES
- 1 APPLE, CORED, SEEDED, AND CUT INTO 8 SLICES

Bring water and juice to a boil over medium heat. Place the tea bags in the mixture, cover, and remove from heat. Let steep 10 minutes, then remove the tea bags. Add the cinnamon. Place 2 cloves in each apple slice and add to tea. Let steep 5 minutes. Pour into mugs, making sure each cup gets 1 apple slice. For an extra touch of style, serve each mug with a cinnamon stick to stir. Serves 8.

❋ CANDLE FIRE ❋

As the weather begins to warm and you no longer use the fireplace, evoke the romance and beauty of a fire by placing four or five pillar candles inside it. The soft light they give off will compensate for the loss of the roaring fire.

❋ CANDIED FLOWERS ❋

These delectable treats are easy to create; use them on top of ice cream or cakes. Pick the flowers fresh in the early morning the day you'll make this.

- **VIOLET BLOSSOMS**
- **ROSE PETALS**
- **1 OR 2 EGG WHITES, DEPENDING ON HOW MANY FLOWERS YOU USE**
- **SUPERFINE SUGAR TO TASTE**

Gently wash flowers and pat dry with a clean towel. Beat the egg whites in a small bowl. Pour the sugar into another bowl. Carefully dip the flowers in the egg whites, then roll in sugar, being sure to cover all sides. Set flowers on a cookie sheet and allow to dry in a warm place. Store in a flat container with waxed paper between layers. The flowers will last for several days.

❋ FLOWER SALADS ❋

Several common flowers are edible—and they add wonderful pops of color and surprising novelty to an ordinary green salad. Not all flowers are edible, though, so make sure the ones you choose are, and wash and thoroughly dry them before using. Common edibles often found in gardens include nasturtiums, roses, borage, marigolds, squash flowers, and violets.

❋ VASEFUL OF JOY ❋

One of the little things in which I regularly find true delight is flower arranging. Although I am not good with my hands (my sister used to leave the house in fear when I was learning to sew in junior high), I do get the urge to make something beautiful, and over the years I have discovered that flower arranging is my creative medium. I don't spend a lot of money—I don't have fancy vases, and I don't buy exotic blooms. I work with whatever is blooming in my garden or selling for a few dollars at the flower stand. At holidays, I may splurge a bit, but I usually use just a few homegrown roses or roadside poppies or a sprig of holly from the tree in

my yard. I have never read a book about the principles
of flower arranging and don't spend too much time
on it—maybe five minutes at the most. For me, the joy
comes from how easy it is to make something pleasing:
selecting an old yellow mustard jar, filling it with
blue cornflowers, and placing it on the kitchen table.
Ongoing beauty meal after meal, in only a few minutes!

❋ SUN TEA ❋

Sun tea is great because it has a mellower flavor than
brewed tea. Drop four tea bags in a quart pitcher of
water—the pitcher must be glass. Cover the pitcher to
keep out bugs and put it outside or on a windowsill in
the full sun. After a few hours, when the sun is hot and
you are too, remove the tea bags. Add ice and serve.
As a variation, try using peach tea. When the tea is
ready, cut up a chilled peach into bite-sized pieces
and add to the tea. Serve immediately for a one-of-a-
kind refresher.

❊ SIMPLE PLEASURES
OF SUMMER ❊

Maybe it's because of our experience of summer vacation as kids, but summer is the season that makes most of us the happiest. Eating outdoors, flowers bursting in yards, swimming, boating, waterskiing, sailing, fresh cherries and nectarines! What are the little things that give you pleasure in the summer? Make a list and be sure to fit them all in this year.

❊ SAND LAMPS ❊

When the weather starts to turn warm and you want to hold an evening garden party, consider this easy-to-make lighting. Simply buy some beautiful terra-cotta pots (or use the ones your plants have grown out of, making sure they are terra-cotta, not plastic). Plug the drain hole of each pot with masking tape, fill it with sand, and insert a fat candle, seating it well in the sand so it stands without wobbling. Shield the candle from the wind with hurricane lamp chimneys. (Safety note: When placing your sand lamps, be certain there is nothing that could easily catch fire nearby.)

❋ BUILD A SANDCASTLE ❋

What fun! All you really need to make a sandcastle is a sandy ocean or lake shore, a few buckets, some shovels and trowels, and some spoons. You'll attract plenty of young helpers. Pick a flat spot where the tide is going out. And don't forget the sunscreen!

❋ SIMPLE SUMMER REFRESHERS ❋

Freeze little slices of lemon or lime into your ice cubes for a pretty and refreshing touch in iced tea or other cold drinks. You can also freeze orange or cranberry juice into ice cubes to add sparkle to lemon–lime soda.

✳ OUTDOOR SHOWERS ✳

One of the best things my mother ever did when we kids
were little was to introduce us to outdoor showers. It
would be a hot sticky summer day in New England, and
suddenly a rainstorm would come up. She would dress
us in our bathing suits and let us run outside. The best
part was standing under the drain spout and letting the
water beat down on our heads. The sense of freedom
and excitement from doing something new, the relief
from the heat and humidity, the peculiar smell of water
meeting superheated asphalt—I can still remember it all
vividly forty years later.

✳ EASY SKIN REFRESHER ✳

I don't know whether I'm so excited about this refresher
because it's so fabulous (which I believe it is) or
because I invented a beauty product on my own. Last
summer, when it was quite hot, I got it into my mind (I
guess because I read that green tea is good for the skin)
to mix equal parts cooled green tea and water in a spray
bottle. I sprayed it all over my face—it felt and smelled
wonderful. I'm hooked on the stuff now.

❋ ICED DELIGHTS ❋

Spice up your ice by adding fruit, herbs, and edible
flowers to the ice trays after you've filled them and
before freezing. They taste great and add a visual kick
to a festive occasion. Here are some fun alternatives
to plain old H_2O: sprigs of fresh rosemary, dill,
lemongrass, or mint; roses, carnations, nasturtiums,
lavender, violets, or pansies (no-spray for sure—do
not use flowers where pesticides have been used);
raspberries, blueberries, cucumber, or the zest of
tangerines, lemon, or lime.

❋ TRADING PLEASURE ❋

Start a bulb-and-seed exchange with friends. When
you are harvesting in the fall—dividing bulbs and drying
out seeds for the next year, try trading with friends as
a no-cost way to increase the variety in your garden.
We started doing this years ago when we found out the
hard way that a packet of zucchini seeds was far too
many for a household of two people. We divided them
up among our friends around the country, and that got
the ball rolling.

To send bulbs, place them in a paper bag and then in a box. To collect seeds, shake the flower heads over an empty glass jar. To send seeds, take a small piece of paper and make a little envelope out of it by folding it in half. Take each side and fold in about a half-inch toward middle. Tape those two sides, place the seeds inside the opening at the top, and then fold top down and tape again. Write on the outside what is inside, and mail in a padded envelope. This also makes a sweet surprise for family or friends.

✳ GIVE YOUR PLANTS A CUP OF TEA ✳

Don't throw leftover herbal tea away—use it to water your houseplants. But be sure it is caffeine-free; plants like tea as long as it is "unleaded."

❊ CANDLE MAGIC ❊

An easy way to make the house cozy in fall is to use
a lot of candles—in the bedroom, living room, dining
room, even in the bathroom. They give a nice glow
to a dark winter evening, and, if scented, also add a
soothing fragrance. The big pillar candles, while nice,
can get pretty expensive, but you can cut down on cost
and customize your own scent by buying inexpensive
unscented votives, pillars, or tea lights at any drugstore.
At home, anoint the candle top with a few drops of your
favorite essential oil—rose, bayberry, and vanilla are
nice—or use your favorite combination for a customized
and affordable scented candle.

You can also decorate candles with herbs and ribbons.
Use large, slow-burning candles and attach small sprigs
or herbs with floral wire or a richly colored ribbon.
Always be sure to place candles on fireproof saucers,
and never leave them unattended!

❋ FEED THE BIRDS ❋

How wonderful to bring birds into your yard by putting out bird feeders. The best time to start is late fall, because the cold weather makes birds more anxious to find food and therefore more willing to try something new. Birds' body temperatures are on average ten degrees warmer than humans, and they need an almost constant food supply to stay alive. The cold weather slows down and kills the insects they eat, so they must find an alternate food supply.

It doesn't matter which side of the house you put the feeder on, but it should be protected from the wind. You should have a good view, but it shouldn't be so active in the room that the birds get scared off. At my parents' house, birds would come when we were sitting quietly, but every time someone moved close to the window, they would scatter. A feeder on a pole in full view of the window but set back a little turned out to be the best compromise at my house. As for the food, wild birdseed mix is fine, as is cracked chick feed mixed with sunflower seeds for the seed-eating birds. Bug eaters such as woodpeckers shy away from seeds but love suet; you can buy special suet feeders at any bird or nature store.

✲ FAVORITE FOODS ✲

At family gatherings, family members can get very particular about their traditional foods. Take some time to make sure you are including the things that speak to your family. Even when I am invited to someone else's house for a family celebration, I always bring my grandmother's cookies because I am so particular about how they are made. What's your simple pleasure when it comes to family foods?

✲ SPICING UP THE FLAMES ✲

The next time you light a fire, sprinkle a few drops of frankincense, cedarwood, or pine essential oil onto a log before lighting it, and you will enjoy an even more fragrant fire.

SELF-CARE LETTER TO READER

Dear Reader,

I hope this book has inspired you to create space for more joy in your busy life. As humans, all we can strive for is to try our best, but in order to try our best, we must take care of ourselves. I believe that when you prioritize your mental, emotional, and spiritual health, you foster a deeper sense of connection with yourself. As we know, everyone practices self-care differently, so I hope to hear from you about what activities best help you to find peace and calm. You are invited to email, tweet, DM, or send a note with your self-care routine or your favorite self-care activity in this book, the one you found to be the most useful.

Thanks for reading—I hope you make time for you today!

XOXO
Becca

ABOUT THE AUTHOR

Becca Anderson comes from a long line of preachers and teachers from Ohio and Kentucky. The teacher side of her family led her to become a woman's studies scholar and the author of *The Book of Awesome Women*. An avid collector of meditations, prayers, and blessings, she helps run a "Gratitude and Grace Circle" virtual circle that meets weekly. In non-pandemic times, she gives gratitude workshops at churches and bookstores in the San Francisco Bay Area, where she currently resides. Becca Anderson credits her spiritual practice with helping her recover from cancer and wants to share this healing wisdom with anyone who is facing difficulty in their life.

Mango Publishing, established in 2014, publishes an eclectic list of books by diverse authors—both new and established voices—on topics ranging from business, personal growth, women's empowerment, LGBTQ studies, health, and spirituality to history, popular culture, time management, decluttering, lifestyle, mental wellness, aging, and sustainable living. We were recently named 2019 *and* 2020's #1 fastest-growing independent publisher by *Publishers Weekly*. Our success is driven by our main goal, which is to publish high-quality books that will entertain readers as well as make a positive difference in their lives.

Our readers are our most important resource; we value your input, suggestions, and ideas. We'd love to hear from you—after all, we are publishing books for you!

Please stay in touch with us and follow us at:
Facebook: Mango Publishing
Twitter: @MangoPublishing
Instagram: @MangoPublishing
LinkedIn: Mango Publishing
Pinterest: Mango Publishing
Newsletter: mangopublishinggroup.com/newsletter

Join us on Mango's journey to reinvent publishing, one book at a time.